Dark Goddess

CRAFT

STEPHANIE WOODFIELD

Dark Goddess

CRAFT

A JOURNEY THROUGH THE
HEART OF TRANSFORMATION

Llewellyn Publications
Woodbury, Minnesota

FIRST EDITION
Fourth Printing, 2020

Cover design by Kevin R. Brown
Interior art by Llewellyn Art Department

Llewellyn Publications is a registered trademark of Llewellyn Worldwide Ltd.

Library of Congress Cataloging-in-Publication Data
Names: Woodfield, Stephanie, author.
  Title: Dark goddess craft : a journey through the heart of transformation /
    Stephanie Woodfield.
  Description: First Edition. | Woodbury : Llewellyn Worldwide, Ltd., 2017. |
    Includes bibliographical references and index.
  Identifiers: LCCN 2017029887 (print) | LCCN 2017041126 (ebook) | ISBN
    9780738754079 (ebook) | ISBN 9780738752563 (alk. paper)
  Subjects: LCSH: Goddesses. | Goddess religion.
  Classification: LCC BL473.5 (ebook) | LCC BL473.5 .W659 2017 (print) | DDC
    202/.114—dc23
  LC record available at https://lccn.loc.gov/2017029887

Llewellyn Worldwide Ltd. does not participate in, endorse, or have any authority or responsibility concerning private business transactions between our authors and the public.
  All mail addressed to the author is forwarded, but the publisher cannot, unless specifically instructed by the author, give out an address or phone number.
  Any Internet references contained in this work are current at publication time, but the publisher cannot guarantee that a specific location will continue to be maintained. Please refer to the publisher's website for links to authors' websites and other sources.

Llewellyn Publications
A Division of Llewellyn Worldwide Ltd.
2143 Wooddale Drive
Woodbury, MN 55125-2989
www.llewellyn.com

Printed in the United States of America

Disclaimer

The publisher and the author assume no liability for any injuries caused to the reader that may result from the reader's use of content contained in this publication and recommend common sense when contemplating the practices described in the work.

Other Books by Stephanie Woodfield

Celtic Lore & Spellcraft of the Dark Goddess: Invoking the Morrigan

Drawing Down the Sun: Rekindle the Magic of the Solar Goddesses

For the Morrigan. I am grateful.

For all the dark goddesses who have touched my life.

For my Tuatha, my Tribe of Ravens. I am grateful for each of you.

For Karen, Gina, Ivy, and Ellie for contributing to this work and being all-around badasses.

For Ed. You are the best man I have ever known. I love you.

Contents

Introduction

It is twilight and I stand in a grassy clearing in a loose circle with others as we celebrate the equinox. Slash pines tower around us, looking like giants in the fading light. It has been a weekend of connecting with old friends and meeting new ones, teaching, and coming together. My spirit feels full and light as my friend leading the ritual tells us to sit, to feel the living ground beneath us, as he begins to walk us through a meditation journey. His voice is calm and soothing, and I follow along easily, slipping into a trance. But there is someone else there in that space between spaces, and she decides she has something different to tell me.

A moment ago I could hear my friend's calm voice. Now it is suddenly gone, as if someone has flipped a switch and muted him, and so is the imagery he was creating. Now I stand in what almost seems like a swamp or a low, quiet lake. The water comes to just below my knees, and it moves slowly among the reeds and tall grass. But this water is as red as blood, and before me stands a woman. I know I am in the river of life and death, the river of the Washer at the Ford. The Washerwoman stands tall and sleek before me, her arms and legs long and willowy like the reeds that surround us. This time she wears a veil over her face; other times her long, black hair falls over her face like a shroud. She stoops over the water and washes something in her hands. I cannot tell if it is a dark garment, the bottom of her own ragged and flowing clothes, or something else entirely. She wrings the garment in her hands, her long, almost clawed fingers running down them and ripping invisible things away.

I have met this face of the Morrigan many times before, but with some trepidation I ask her what message she has for me. She points further out into the water, which has no shore and seems to go onward in every direction forever. The water begins to ripple, starting at my feet and moving forward into the distance. And then I begin to see the ritual circle that I sit in again, the solid ground beneath me, and the two images merge. The ground, which seemed so unmovable before, is nothing but rippling water—fluid, changeable, and reshapeable as the ripples move through them.

"Nothing can withstand the change I bring. Do you understand?" The ripples in the water are small but they feel like a tsunami. I feel the force of them washing through me, and I feel compelled to walk forward through the waters, the ripples changing everything around me and propelling me forward at the same time in an unstoppable wave. "You have asked me for change. You have set the wheel in motion. Nothing can stop this now, not even you." And I know she is right. I have begun to make changes in my life, ones whose consequences I know will reshape my life. But this is the kind of reshaping that involves buildings crumpling and the ground beneath my feet being pulled away. If I do what I need to do, I will have to destroy so many things in my life and see what I can rebuild out of the rubble. But the cost of not doing this would be even greater.

Still pulled onward by the river, I turn to see the Washerwoman walking beside me. It is hard to see her face behind the veil of wet hair. What stands out are her bloodstained lips and the words she speaks, which move through me like the rippling water: "Remember that you are worthy. This will come to pass. No man or god can stop it now."

And then the river and the Washerwoman are gone. I see just the darkness behind my closed eyes, hear the calm, soothing voice of my friend as he continues to guide the others through the meditation. I take a breath and try to ground myself. I put a hand on the ground and run my fingers through the grass. The ground is solid, but I still feel the shadow of the rippling water.

I went home from that festival feeling grateful for the Washerwoman's message and determined to make the changes that over the last two years I had been coming to terms with and working through in many different ways. Change can be a slow process; little things lead you in unexpected directions. And other times change can be as quick and cutting as a sword. I didn't expect my life to fall apart, regardless of me initiating the changes, the very next day after my flight landed. But it did. And the Washerwoman had been right. I had laid the groundwork, and on some level I was convinced she had as well, for the things that happened. I ended an eleven-year relationship, I nearly found myself homeless, and I was reminded that blood family isn't always family. I learned that I had some amazing friends, I moved across the country, and I learned that I did deserve happiness. Just because I could try to hold up the weight of the world didn't mean I had to or was supposed to. I had to learn to feel, and own, my own self-worth.

Nothing was easy about these changes; nothing ever is with the Morrigan. But I don't regret it, and it was worth it in the end. She is not the only dark goddess who has challenged me or dug her claws into my soul and made her mark, and she will not be the last. As painful as that part of my life was, I cannot help but be grateful. Life is about changing and growing, about tearing away and learning and relearning who we are and who we can be. It's never easy, and it isn't supposed to be. The dark goddesses that have walked by my side during such times have wrapped black wings around me, mourned alongside me the pieces of myself that were no more, and at times forced me to get up and fight. For that I will always be grateful. Sometimes their lessons came easily; other times they were a painful process. But I always emerged stronger in the end and with a greater understanding of myself.

Working and building a devotion to dark deities can be a rewarding process—and an utterly life changing one. If you feel called to dark and dangerous gods, don't be afraid to embrace the path and to challenge what you think you know and how you practice. Follow the gods into the dark and be transformed. You may cry and scream and rage along the way, but you'll never feel more alive and your life will transform for the better.

Part 1
Who Is the Dark Goddess?

It's time to get started. It's time to wake up.
Don't wait another minute.
Claim your heart, and claim your glory.
You have all you need.
—Marianne Williamson, *A Woman's Worth*

We call her the Crone, the goddess of the underworld, goddess of death, the dark goddess. She rules over everything that we fear. She offers us wisdom in exchange for pain. She is the Morrigan, inciting her favored warriors into frenzy on the battlefield. She is the Washer at the Ford, keening while she washes the bloody clothes of those destined to die. She is Hekate, who lights our way through the underworld. She is the terrifying Kali, who dances with abandon on the corpses of her enemies, wearing their severed heads as ornamentation, and she is Sekhmet, who drinks blood like wine. She is sometimes terrifying, her lessons often painful, but the dark goddess dwells within each of us and is a vital part of our being. She is the force that shines within us in our darkest hour and the face we turn to when we seek rebirth. She likes nothing better than to break us apart, only to remake us anew.

The dark goddess and the lessons she teaches are vital to our lives. Her destructive aspects teach us that there is death within life, that we are constantly changing and evolving. No matter what we have been through in our lives, we can rise from the ashes and like Kali dance ecstatically on the ruins of our old selves toward rebirth. As the fierce warrior drinking the blood of the slain, she is a no-nonsense goddess, teaching us to make our voices heard, to stand up and be counted, and inspiring us to bring about change, both in ourselves and the world around us. And she is also the shadowy keeper of the dead, teaching us how to pierce the veil, to see into the future, and to commune with the beloved dead. But she is also the side of the Divine that we avoid the most, and as a consequence we often have difficulty working with her.

Dark gods rule over the things we fear the most. Some fear that working with this aspect of the dark goddess will bring out the darkest or worst parts of themselves. Other times we are simply afraid to welcome change into our lives and finally release the things we keep buried deep within our souls. While working with the darker aspects of the Goddess may make you face things about yourself you would rather ignore, her path is one of transformation and ultimately one of healing.

But where do we begin? How do we look past our fear and understand how to work with dark deities? My friend Gina will tell you that she thinks some people should have to take a test before they can work with goddesses like Hekate, the Morrigan, or Kali. I remember laughing at the idea as we sat around a bonfire in her yard one summer night, talking about how seeking out and working with dark goddesses had affected each of our lives and how others around us were affected by the touch of such gods. But then I really thought about it. These goddesses have a habit of turning your life upside down, breaking down barriers, and bringing about needed but often painful transformation. Some who dive headfirst into the realm of the dark goddess, they may find themselves overwhelmed, frustrated, and oftentimes stuck. We lose our way in the dark and don't quite know how to grope our way through the underworld and shadowlands we find ourselves in or how to face the challenges given to us. The dark goddess has a habit of hammering lessons into our flesh until we have truly understood and worked through them. When we ask the gods for change, they are more than willing to give it to us, but we aren't always ready to go through that process of transformation. But if it were an easy process, it wouldn't be meaningful.

Maybe we don't so much need a test but a manual. A guide through the dark, a torch to light our way through the underworld, to give those who seek transformation a tool kit. It is my hope that this book will be just that: your guide through the dark, not only a guide to who the dark goddess is but how to work with her, how to approach the work she gives us, bring true transformation into your life, and navigate safely through her realm.

In the first part of this book we will look at who the dark goddess really is, misconceptions surrounding dark deities, and how to go about transformation and devotional work. Throughout the rest of the book, we will work in depth with goddesses from multiple pantheons as we move through our own journey of transformation. You will find spells and meditations as well as workings to aid you in your journey. You will also find a few spells and invocations from the members of the Tuatha Dé Morrigan, a group with whom I have explored and honored dark deity, hosted retreats, and held public ritual for the last several years. As each of these individuals has had unique and significant experiences with the goddesses we will be working with, I offer their perspectives and include tools and techniques that these seasoned practitioners have used with success.

Dark Goddess Craft is about delving into our own darkness and emerging renewed. It is learning how to dance in the void, knowing when to let certain aspects of our lives go, and making room for the new. It is a path of transformation, change, and healing. It is the art of learning to confront your shadows and truly discovering who you are. The dark goddess, in all her many faces and guises, stands at the threshold of the otherworlds, waiting for us to learn her mysteries. Torch in hand, she waits to guide us through our inner darkness and lead us to rebirth. Will you follow her into the dark?

1

THE NATURE OF DARK GODS

When I first begin working with a deity, there is a certain kind of protocol I go through. It is the same whether or not I have chosen to connect to that particular god or they have, as gods so often do, just appeared out of the blue making demands in my life. The gods are very real to me. They are vibrant beings with their own personalities, tastes, likes, and dislikes. They move through my life like old friends and, at times, unexpected strangers. When you have heard the laugh of the Morrigan, it is impossible to confuse her for Cerridwen or Hekate. The heat and coppery taste of Eris's energy is nothing like the fire that fuels Kali's dance. The vastness of Hekate's presence is not the same as that of Ereshkigal. They are all very distinct from one another. And getting to know a god is not unlike the processes we go through when we build a relationship with a new friend or lover. You begin to learn that person's personality. With the gods, I start by learning the myths of those particular deities and about the cultures they originate from. I make altars, I make offerings, and I do journey work to connect with them. It's important to understand the nature of the god you plan on working with. Ultimately, I trust my gods. They are not strangers to me. Sometimes I don't know where they are leading me. I may face their challenges willingly or go kicking and screaming, but there is trust between us. Because there is a long-standing, deep relationship there.

To work with dark gods requires that we delve into their nature. We will work closely with the individual goddesses and their myths, but first it is important to understand how dark deities as a whole function: who they are, how we have come to view them, and the processes they rule over. There are pitfalls and challenges to working with any deity, and there seems to be a consistent pattern to the challenges many of us run into when working with dark gods. And I think some of these arise because of how we are taught to approach the gods and how we have been taught to view change.

Dark versus Light

What exactly does it mean when we refer to a goddess or god as "dark"? Is this the darkness of the night sky? The void? The darkness where monsters live under the bed? Or for that matter, what do we mean by "light"? Humans have a tendency to want to put things as vast and unknowable as the Divine into boxes, to categorize and simplify them, in an attempt to understand them better. We label things in our search for understanding. It's human nature. In modern Paganism we often divide deities into two camps: dark and light. Essentially, the idea of a god or goddess being dark or light is a modern one. It has no real place in ancient culture. Gods in every pantheon have always specialized in certain areas, whether that be agriculture, healing, or ruling the underworld. But in general that is where the categorizing ended for our ancestors. Dividing the Divine into dualistic, often opposing natures is very much in line with our modern concepts of good and evil and stems from the influence of monotheistic religion. Today we like to think of the world in terms of everything having its opposite, instead of seeing that most things, including the gods, fall into a gray area. There is male and female, night and day, and good and evil. Dark deities are in no way evil, but what we have learned to do when we approach the gods in this manner is to label any deity that holds sway over a realm or concept that frightens us as "dark." Gods who rule over death, change, war, violence, anger, and all the things that make life difficult or painful must also be dangerous and untrustable in some way, not unlike the things they hold sway over. What we often fail to see is that dark gods are not the cause of these things, but rather the very beings who teach us to understand them, who challenge us to move past our fears and give us the strength to face some of the more painful unavoidable things in life.

The deities we label as "dark" today would not have been viewed as malevolent by our ancestors. The things modern people tend to have hang-ups about are more removed from the lives of the ancient people who worshiped these gods. To our ancestors deities like Mars or the Morrigan would be the kind of gods you wanted on your side if you were fighting a war or you were concerned for the safety of your village and family.

We don't have to worry about invaders coming from the next town or apartment building to steal our food stores for the winter. In the past a war goddess on your side was a
very good thing. To ancient people the gods we tend to treat with fear today would have
been essential to their everyday lives. And conversely, the gods we tend to fear in modern
times may not be so scary to our descendants. Maybe in three hundred years Aphrodite
will be considered a dark goddess—who knows?

Defining "dark" as a term that always indicates something negative also has racial
connotations. There is an element of cultural baggage around the idea that lightness is
good or preferable and being darker is shameful when it comes to skin color. There is
even a myth about how Parvati is shamed by another god who calls her dark-skinned,
and she takes measures to lighten her appearance, the darkness she sheds transforming
into the goddess Kali, whose name means "black." We have to let go of the idea that
"dark," within any context, is a bad thing. These attitudes influence not just the way we
look at each other but how we perceive deity.

The concept of gods of light is just as modern and at times rather misleading. We
tend to assume that gods who do not deal with the things we fear all have motherly, loving traits to them. At times I have found Brighid, who by modern standards fits this mold
of being connected to light, to be just as challenging to work with as any dark goddess.
She has her motherly side, yes, but her fires can burn you just as easily as they can spark
inspiration. It is best to not assume to know the full nature of a god.

Ultimately, I prefer not to categorize the gods. They are all very distinct from one
another. They are multifaceted. Just as I am many things to many people, so too are the
gods. You may be a parent, a spouse, a child, and a coworker and play many roles to different people, but you are still one person. When we put a label on something, we tend
to forget that it is anything else but the label we have given it. It took me many years to
see that the Morrigan has other aspects and faces. She can be dark and scary, but that
is not the limit of her power or scope as a deity. The problem with labeling something
"dark" or "light" is that we put blinders on and forget that the gods are more than the
title or box people put them in.

Throughout this book, I will refer to the goddesses we are working with as "dark," but
only because this has evolved into the terminology that we are most familiar with. I use
the term "dark" only in the context of a grouping of deities that have similar functions

relating to transformation. I suggest you take time to consider what the terms "light" and "dark" mean to you personally. Consider if thinking of the gods in these terms has limited your experiences with them and if you are comfortable using or discarding this terminology.

Are All Dark Goddesses Crones?

Terms like "dark" or "light" are ultimately just generalizations, and with them come certain stigmas. In general when we are talking about a dark goddess, it is almost always assumed that we are also talking about a crone. While the archetypal Neopagan Crone is connected to death and some of the harsher mysteries the Goddess embodies, the two are not mutually exclusive. In pantheons around the world we find maiden and mother goddesses whose energies and lessons challenge us and teach us the mysteries of transformation and rebirth. We tend to relegate the happier and more appealing aspect of the Divine Feminine to the Maiden and Mother and pack all the darker and uncomfortable things into the Crone's corner. While the Crone is certainly connected to death and transformation, the myths and stories of goddesses around the world show us that the Maiden and Mother figures also have a darker side. Hekate, who is more often than not portrayed in modern art as a hag or crone, is shown as three young maidens in early Greek art. The concept that she appears only as an elderly woman is a fairly modern one, fitting our preconceived image of what a deity that deals with death and the underworld should look like. Likewise, Persephone, who descends into the underworld for half the year and rules as its queen, is a maiden figure who deals with transitions and the world of the dead. Sedna and the Welsh Blodeuwedd are also both young goddess figures who face difficult times and embody the independence and self-ownership the dark goddess embodies.

This idea that only the Crone can embody the darker side of the feminine is why when the discussion of dark gods in general comes up within Paganism, it is often assumed that one is exclusively talking about male deities. The lessons and nature of a god have nothing to do with gender. There are many dark gods that are powerful allies to work with as well—Hades, Ares, and Crom Dubh to name a few. Part of why I chose to center my focus here on dark goddesses is because they are often ignored. We have acquired an aversion to seeing femininity as a force of powerful, destructive change. But just as the concept of being a "nurturer" is not exclusively female, the concepts of strong action and destruction are not exclusively in the masculine realm either. We need to question why we automatically pigeonhole a goddess that appears as maiden in her myths or one that just so happens to be a mother to certain relegated roles. The Irish Macha is a mother, and one of her central myths involves how she birthed her twins. But she also goes off to war, fights in battles, and is known for her prophetic visions and eye for strategy. So is she a mother goddess simply because she bore children—case closed, end of story? Or is she something more, just as Persephone is more than simply a maiden?

Are Dark Gods Dangerous?

The idea that a god is dangerous doesn't sit well with many people, and this is perhaps the biggest reason many Pagans shy away from working with dark gods. The deities we classify as dark are those who deal with or rule over the harsher, scarier parts of life. They are the sin-eaters, those who rule over the land of the dead or usher spirits into the next world, those connected to the violence of war, those who have faced brutality in their myths, and those who rule over liminal and transformational space. Deities like this challenge us. They shake up our lives when they appear and force us to look at all the things that are uncomfortable about life and ourselves. In short they are not happy mother goddesses who will pat us on the head and tell us everything will be okay. Instead they are more likely to put a sword in our hands and tell us, like the Spartans, to come home with our shields in hand or laid on top of us. In short they represent many of the things we are afraid of. And there is nothing more terrifying to most people than change.

It's no wonder we are often reluctant to work with such gods, but more often than not their transformational powers are exactly what we need in our lives. Ten years ago saying the Morrigan's name at a Pagan gathering was like saying "Voldemort." She was "that scary goddess," and I was often advised not to work with her. Now the Morrigan is one of the most talked-about and popular deities in Celtic Paganism. To those who have answered her call she can be a source of strength and power. She is not the only dark goddess whose worship has gained momentum. Slowly we are starting to rethink how we approach deities we have dubbed to be "dark." Ultimately, working with these deities is a process of transformation in itself. Even though the concept of labeling deities as "dark" or "light" is modern, walking the path of the dark goddess is not the same as working with other deities. Working with deities that bring about change and represent our own fears can be challenging. No matter what label I put on the Morrigan, she is still the Morrigan. And she is very, very good at making me face the things I'd rather hide from.

So are the gods dangerous? Well, the short answer is yes. And when you get down to it, isn't living dangerous too? Taking the subway or getting in your car can be dangerous, but it's a kind of risk or danger that you accept. Working with dark and dangerous gods can be like that. Life is not without risks any more than magick, working with the gods, or, for that matter, working with other spiritual beings is. Consider what any good teacher will tell you about faeries or even angels. Most will advise you that caution is required when working with these beings. The Sídhe are not Tinker Bell. They can be beneficial or try to eat you. For the most part, no one has any qualms about labeling faeries as dangerous. After all, they can be at times. But it also doesn't negate that having a connection to them and working with them can be rewarding. The danger is understood. We understand that although many of the Sídhe have humanlike appearances, they are inherently not human. They are something different and distinct from us, and we can't expect them to play by human rules or have human moralities. Likewise, with angels there is an understanding that they are not human. And if you have read the traditional descriptions of angels (they resemble fat little winged babies about as much as the Sídhe resemble Tinker Bell), you'll find they can be quite scary. Some have thousands of eyes or animal heads and rain down the wrath of God with pleasure. But again we have an easier time accepting the danger and the understanding that some are beneficial and others we may have to be wary about or take certain precautions with.

Coming from monotheism, many of us were raised with the idea of a "heavenly father" watching over us. It is a concept many of us carry over into Paganism. When viewing the gods as creators of the universe and ourselves, it's only natural to equate our relationships with them to the closest human equivalent we have, our parents. The only hang-up with this is that when we see the gods as parental figures, our next conclusion is that they love us unconditionally. The problem is no matter how human they appear or what form they take, the gods are powers so vast and unknowable that our human minds can't really completely comprehend them. They created stars and planets, us, and all the beings we share this planet with. I do think the gods care about us and aspects of our lives, but at the same time I think they also have their own agendas and have a much vaster picture in mind. We can't apply human expectations to them—or moralities, for that matter. We want them to be human, but really they are not. That is not to say they are not a part of us, and I feel we are a part of them. There is a connection, an interaction between us, but that is not the same thing. The Sídhe and angels may appear humanlike, yet by definition they are something completely different from us. When working with dark gods, we forget that they will make us face uncomfortable things. Asking for their help may land us in situations we may not like, even if overall it will lead us to be stronger or to overcome something. When we are faced with that kind of tough love, it's not hard to see how dark gods get labeled as "evil" or "dangerous" because they don't quite fit the loving heavenly parent image. A deity may well love us, but if they think making your world come crashing down is what's best for you or what you have asked them for, they will have no qualms about making it part of your reality.

We can't see the gods as spiritual parents who never get mad at us. Gods can and do get mad at people. And usually you get the pointy end of the stick pretty quick when it happens. Not showing respect to the gods and treating them like spiritual vending machines when we want something can have consequences. Asking them for help and not really wanting to do the work can be dangerous too. You can't expect the gods to wave a wand and make everything better. They will help you but you have to earn it. And you have to be willing to bleed a little sometimes.

When some people discuss their work with the Morrigan, or gods like her, they will often describe a whole lot of upheaval and crap happening when they asked her to help them bring some kind of change into their lives. The Morrigan will goad you, throw you off the deep end, so to speak. She will place things in your path until you have truly dealt with your demons. It's not to say she won't help you—she will—but it isn't in her nature to give you the easy way out. Similarly, a friend who works with Odin has said to me in the past that if you give Odin an inch, he will take a mile. Knowing that this is how these gods operate is vital to working with them. Knowing their personalities can help when working with them and help you set boundaries when dealing with them. When I work with Odin, I know that being very clear about things is important because if I'm not, it will be like talking to a genie, and my words may be twisted in ways that fit Odin's agenda best. With the Morrigan I know that I have to really want the things I ask of her and that they are worth the pain they will most likely cost me. I also know that the Morrigan is direct, while Hekate, for example, will lead me to a revelation in a slower, slightly gentler way, like walking a winding path versus base jumping. Knowing these things changes how I approach them, both in ritual and personal practice.

The next logical question is "Are they too dangerous to work with?" My answer to that is no. But like working with faeries or other beings, we must approach the work with some understanding that there is a certain element of risk. The gods will challenge you, make you stronger than you have ever been, but at the same time they can completely rearrange your life. Sometimes it can be exactly what we need. But when we ask them for things, we must realize risk is involved. We may have to let go of other things to achieve the things we want, to become the kind of person we wish to be. All magic comes at a price.

My relationship with and devotion to the dark gods I work with is deep, and there is great love there, on both ends, I think. It's a relationship that has built and grown over many years. But I can't see them as spiritual mothers who will wipe my ass either. We have to let go of that image of the gods. That idea of God the Father way up in the clouds looking down benevolently on his children doesn't always apply to the gods. And it truthfully doesn't describe the Old Testament's image of Yahweh either.

Dark gods can be dangerous; working with them has consequences and rewards. We must remember that these are vast and powerful beings. They are not human, not truly. No matter how close to humanity they are, they are still something different.

2

WORKING WITH DARK DEITIES

Now that we have looked at the nature of dark gods and how they might differ from other deities, the next step is to examine how to approach working with them. Before we delve into working with specific dark gods, we must look at some of the basics of interacting with these deities. Working with a deity in general is something we should not rush headlong into without following some basic protocols. Interacting with every god is different, but in general there are some considerations that apply to most of the gods we think of as dark deities. Forging a relationship with a deity can have its pitfalls and complications. It is something we have to work at like any other relationship.

Devotional Practice

Devotional practice is the art of honoring and connecting to deity, usually through offerings, prayers, and other acts of devotion. Galina Krasskova describes devotional practice as being the "heart" of our Pagan traditions, and I can't agree more. She goes on to describe the art of devotion as the following:

> This is what makes our faiths live and grow and what infuses them with joy and what opens doors for our Gods to come through.... Devotion then is that which ones cultivates to develop and maintain right relationship with the Holy powers....
>
> ... Devotion is a personal thing and when you do it well, and engage with the Gods in whatever way you're able to, you'll find it takes on a life of its own.[1]

---

1. Galina Krasskova, *Devotional Polytheism: An Introduction* (Sanngetall Press, 2014), p. 1.

Devotional practice is a very personal thing, and at times because it is such a personal and individual endeavor, it can be difficult to develop a road map for yourself in this arena. The particular offerings and acts of a devotee will vary depending on the person and the deity they are honoring. How two people go about honoring Oya may vary greatly. One might use traditional offerings, while another may feel they are drawn to offer a specific thing the deity indicates they want. Yet another devotee of the same deity may spend more time in prayer and meditation than pouring offerings. The key to devotional work is the manner in which you go about it. If you approach it as a chore or see offerings as just so much wine being poured out into a cup rather than a gift and communion with deity, then the libation will do nothing for you.

Devotional practice is also more than pouring out offerings. It creates a bridge between you and deity. It is offering a portion of your day, a portion of your time focusing on that relationship and nurturing it. It also allows you time to speak with deity. Our lives are often busy and chaotic, and it's hard sometimes to turn off the noise and really listen to what the Divine may be trying to tell us.

For many, the first time they encounter a deity might be in a group or public ritual. Perhaps it's Imbolc and the priestess or person leading the ritual is invoking Brighid or welcoming her into the space for that particular celebration. What often isn't discussed is that the person invoking or welcoming the deity to the space has more than likely done some homework beforehand to be able to facilitate that experience and create a connection to the deity in question. It is vital when working with a deity to first do some research on that deity, meditate, build a connection to them, and learn their likes or dislikes. All these things encompass devotional work. If you didn't do them, it would be like knocking on your neighbor's door and asking to borrow butter when you have never been properly introduced or spoken to them before. It isn't very different with gods. Although the person facilitating the ritual may seem like they are effortlessly drawing in and connecting to deity, more than likely they have spent at the very least the last few weeks or months doing devotional work with that deity.

A good first step to devotional work is to create a space or an altar for the deity you will be working with. This can be something small, like a spot on a bookshelf to place a small picture or an item that represents that deity. It can function as a place you can go to consciously connect with this deity, leave offerings, and in general welcome that deity's presence into your life. Your altar can be as simple or extravagant as you like: it could be a corner of a bookshelf, a section of your nightstand, a floating shelf (these make really excellent altars), or a shrine that takes up a whole wall.

Learning the mythology and traditions that surround a deity sounds like common sense, but it is a critical aspect of devotional practice. And you will be surprised how many people don't bother to do it. This doesn't mean you have to become an expert or follow a particular custom when working with that deity, but it can give you a background of the things you may encounter when working with that god and how you might approach them. There may also be practices or taboos surrounding a deity that you should be aware of. For example, in one of Yemayá's myths, she was poisoned, and some devotees hold it as proper protocol to taste whatever is being offered to the goddess first before leaving it as an offering, to show that the offering is good to eat. Would lightning come out of the sky if you didn't observe this practice? Probably not, but doing so deepens your devotion and gives you a rhyme and reason to your devotional acts. The deity you are forging a relationship with may not have any taboos or particular protocol, but knowing their mythology can help you come up with meaningful ways for you to honor them.

Asking the deity what they would like is also important. It may not even be a particular offering but a certain action or show of respect. I know two devotees of Hekate who both felt the goddess wanted them to be veiled or have their heads covered when doing devotional work at their home altars. It was something the deity nudged them toward rather than something they found in ancient practices or from a modern tradition. Neither knew the other, but both mentioned the practice to me at different times and found it validating to know someone else had felt directed to honor Hekate in the same way. Even if it is not something you find in the lore surrounding a deity, listening to the Divine and crafting your own practices with them can be very fulfilling. Trusting your gut and the relationship between yourself and deity is really the best thing to do that situation.

Consider your offering. Why have you chosen this particular offering? Does it have meaning for you? Do you feel the deity accepts the offering? If you can answer yes to those questions, then use it.

Once you have created a space to honor deity and found offerings you wish to leave, the real work begins. How do you connect to deity? How do you forge a relationship? The answer is different for everyone. You might want to do journey work to meet and encounter deity or leave offerings and sit quietly and see what messages come to you. You might want to simply sit by your altar space and talk to deity like you would your best friend.

Offerings

The kinds of offerings you choose to give a deity will vary. You will find that dark gods ask for certain types of things or are traditionally associated with being given particular kinds of offerings. Liquor tends to be the most common type of offering, and I'm not above admitting I've wandered around a liquor store until I felt a nudge from a certain deity as to what they would like.

Alcohol or food offerings are not the limit to what can be given to the gods. While I do regularly pour libations, the most meaningful offerings that I choose to give the gods are often not material things. I might offer a particular task as an offering. Whether that is creating something or doing something, I approach the entire thing as a kind of ritual offering to deity. One of my first teachers would often say, "Do something tomorrow that you were afraid to do today." Many of the things I offered the Morrigan when I first encountered her involved this. "I will do this thing that frightens me, in your honor." It is not something that should be blindly done. I usually formally offer the task to the deity in question, and there is usually a conversation that goes along with it, a sort of negotiation.

I have also been known to carry around emergency offerings for when I'm not at home or traveling, both in my car and in my purse. A condiment packet of honey from a coffee shop or the small plastic creamers served in diners are excellent on-the-go offerings. They may not be very extravagant offerings, but they work well in a pinch. All that really matters is the spirit in which the offering is given.

Another stigma attached to honoring dark gods is that you will be asked to offer them things you are uncomfortable with. Offerings are very personal things, and while one person may find deep meaning in a particular item they are offering, another may find it repugnant. At times people become concerned that they are not offering a deity the "correct" thing if another person does not use the same or similar offerings. Usually, it's our own moral tastes that come into play here. One devotee might offer a fine cut of raw meat to a deity, while another who is vegetarian might view the act as dishonorable. Who is right and who is wrong? Well, neither. If the person is offering meat in a devotional way, it has meaning to them, and they felt the gods accepted it, then good for them. The vegetarian devotee might find something else that has meaning for them and that they are comfortable with. Neither's choice in offerings is correct or incorrect. This can also be said of offering blood to a deity (covered this in more detail in chapter 5). If you have had issues with self-harming in the past or are just uncomfortable with the idea, then find something else that works for you. There are no right or wrong answers with offerings; what matters the most is your connection to deity and the spirit in which you make the offering. Trusting your gut and the relationship between you and deity is really the best thing to consider when you are unsure of an offering. A good rule of thumb is:

1. Why have you chosen this particular offering?

2. Does it have meaning for you?

3. Do you feel the deity accepted the offering?

When Things Get Hairy

Like any kind of magick, things can and do go wrong at times. Working with dark gods is no different. Transformation and the lessons of the gods do have consequences, beyond personal change through the process of working with them. Many people tend to look at gods as heavenly parents and assume that as such they always have our best interests in mind. "Parent" is the closest thing we can really equate a god to, but it doesn't nearly describe the interaction a devotee has with a deity or the true nature of a deity for that matter. Gods are vast. They are old. In my personal experience they are always ten steps ahead of you, as they should be—they are gods, after all. And they have their own agendas, which are usually far vaster and wider ranging than our own.

So how can things go wrong? Well, there are actually quite a few ways.

First off, don't make promises you can't keep. Especially to the gods. This issue can manifest in a number of ways. If you make an oath to a deity, in ritual or otherwise, expect to keep it. Our words not only have power, but they also have consequences. If you avoid your oath or don't do what you have promised, don't be surprised when things start going poorly for you. Don't wait for the cosmic smackdown before beginning to fulfill your word. Also, when you enter a relationship with a deity, if you feel they want you to do something for them or you wish to offer a task or devotional act to them, give a clear time frame. The deity may not care that you don't have the time, money, or resources to finish that task, only that you promised to fulfill it.

Similarly, you may feel a deity wants you to do a certain task or kind of work for them. Before entering into any kind of oath, it's important to remember you can negotiate. A deity might really want you to work on a specific thing. But you still have needs too, and that task may seem all-consuming or impossible. You need a job that pays the bills and a roof over your head. There is nothing wrong with negotiation, in asking the gods for what we need as well. For example, a friend felt a certain deity was calling her to do healing work (okay, maybe "demanding" is a better word), particularly counseling, but she found the more she tried to do the work the less she was able to keep the rest of her life afloat. Mostly, she stretched herself thin trying to uphold the work she felt she needed to do for that deity and the rest of her life, and she was draining herself in the process. As part of an oath to that deity, she asked that she find a job where she could do work in honor of that deity but also have enough to make ends meet and be stable in her own life. A few months later she found a job that paid well and was able to do the counseling work she felt called to. Building a devotional relationship with any deity is never going to be a one-way conversation. Negotiation and not working on blind faith are important.

Another hang-up, oddly enough, is getting what you want. When you ask a deity for something, really understand what it is you are asking for. A long time ago I made a vow to the Morrigan to find my own happiness and asked her to help me in doing so. Sounds easy, right? Keeping that oath is probably one of the hardest things I have ever taken on—and the most rewarding. It forced me to face a lot of difficult choices. There were things in my life that weren't good for me, yet I still clung to them. I didn't quite expect to be made to look squarely and honestly at those things when I made that vow. I naively expected just to feel happier about life in general and learn to be happy with what I had, instead of facing the fact that things in my life, not simply my outlook, actually had to change for me to be happy. I actually had to do work. I also didn't expect the process to be as painful as it was. But I did get exactly what I asked for. And while it did turn out well, it was not an easy process. As magick users, we know words have power. Our oaths to the gods are no less powerful than words of power or words uttered to weave a spell, and thus they cannot be taken lightly or dispensed carelessly.

Perhaps the most uncomfortable pitfall is when a god turns their back on you, so to speak. It does happen. As much as we want to see the gods as all loving parents, sometimes those "parents" get fed up with our shit. Usually this occurs when you haven't been listening to a deity. There is only so much divine foot tapping and arm folding a god can do before leaving you to stew in your own juices. They leave you there to figure things out for yourself. They stop talking to you when you aren't carrying out your part of the bargain.

How do you fix things? Make offerings. And listen! If you are asking for answers, what is the deity telling you? If you have trouble meditating and receiving messages, then use other media: cards, runes, and so on. If the problem stems from an oath that has been broken, follow through with the promise to the best of your abilities. Acknowledge that you messed up and ask for aid in accomplishing the task or understanding how to do so.

Things can also go wrong when we only make offerings or do devotional work when we want something. If you create an altar for Kali, pay attention to it only when you want something or when things start hitting the fan, and ignore it and the deity the rest of the time, you will not likely get the most positive outcome. Building a connection and relationship is important and shouldn't revolve around only doing the work and building the connection in times of need. I find this to be particularly true of working with the Sídhe and spirits. The gods are no different.

3

CURSING, WARDING, AND
OTHER DEFENSIVE MAGICK

While our main focus will be how to work with dark deities in order to transform our lives, it is important to be able to protect ourselves along the journey. There is a healthy respect for and tradition of using curses and defensive magick in Santería and Hoodoo traditions. But when it comes to modern Witchcraft as a whole, we tend to shy away from it. Reconstructionists and those in traditions that do not hold to the Wiccan Rede are less shy about such things, but still as a whole Pagans should put more of an emphasis on learning magickal defense and offense. Protection and retribution are certainly in the realm of dark gods, and you can use the techniques in this chapter with any of the goddesses in this book.

Let me start out by saying I don't believe in the "harm none" axiom. It's an impossible idea. I do believe that we should be good to one another and live well and honorably. But I do not think those two words really sum up a moral code for the Craft or Paganism in general. If you ate a hamburger recently or picked a pretty flower from the garden, you have broken this law. Our very existence cannot be without harming or destroying something. That ultimately is the ever-swaying pendulum of balance. Something gets destroyed to fuel something else, and then the cycle continues on and on. If we tried to harm nothing in our existence, we would inevitably harm ourselves in our efforts in trying to do so, starving and allowing others to treat us poorly in lieu of protecting ourselves. This holds true in magick as well. You just can't banish someone in a nice way. It just doesn't work. When you need someone to get the hell away to keep yourself and others around you safe, it's not always going to be pretty. We have to become comfortable with the idea of force, rather than the implied passivity of adhering to the ideas behind the rede. Most people would agree that if someone physically attacked you, you have every right to fight back. That same idea applies to magick. If someone has sent some nasty energy your way, you have every right to magickally push right back.

This does not mean we should not lead our lives by a moral code, nor does it mean that we should not have morals in regard to our magickal practices. Rather, it's that each person's morals are ultimately for themselves to flesh out and adhere to. That being said, there are plenty of people out in the world who don't wish us well. And it's imperative to be able to defend against such people or against unwanted and negative beings. After all, not every faery wants to help us; some of them want to eat your face off. And not every human is good natured.

Modern Pagans have hang-ups regarding cursing in particular. If we look to the pagans of the past, we see they had fewer issues with asking the gods to curse others for them. Temples in continental Europe and Roman-Celtic ones in Britain have many examples of curse tablets offered to gods by those seeking justice for minor things, such as stolen shoes, and for more heinous crimes.

Warding

Warding is perhaps one of the most important things you can do magickally to protect yourself and your home, not just from unwanted people but also from unwanted spirits and beings. There are several ways to go about creating wards and placing them in your home. You might create one to protect your home in general, another for your ritual space and the things you do there, and one in your car to protect you while you are away from home.

Simple House Ward

Before erecting wards, I like to smudge my house and use a little water with a pinch of salt in it to draw an X in the corners of all the doorways, windows, and mirrors, just as a general cleansing before I start my work. Wards are not something you do once and forget about. They are something you feed and add power to as time goes on, like recharging batteries. You can create them purely through visualization, but I like to have a physical object to anchor the energy into. In this case, we will use four crystals or stones of your choice that will be placed in the four corners of the home. You can use more than four, as some people prefer to have enough stones to keep in all the windowsills and near entryways. While you can literally place the stones in the actual corners of the home, I like to use a drawing on the layout of the home as a kind of grid to place the stones on. If you live in an apartment complex, you can even print out a floor plan from your rental company's website. This is just as effective and makes it easier to keep track of the stones when you want to give them an extra energy charge every so often. If you have curious pets, it is also a good way to keep the stones from becoming playthings. The drawing of the home's layout is also a focal point for your visualization.

You Will Need:
Four stones or crystals
Drawing or representation of your home
Salt
Water

Hold the stones in your hands and look at your drawing. Clearly see the boundaries of your home in your mind's eye. See a grid work of light shooting out of the stones, creating a web of light that protects your home and sends away those who are unwanted or wish you harm. Alternatively, you could see a grid of vines with large thorns surrounding the home from top to bottom sending back anything that is unwanted. If you come up with another visualization you prefer better, use it. Also, be very clear about what is allowed to come into your space and what you want to repel. When you feel your intent is clearly imbued in the stones, set them on the four corners of the picture (or the four corners of your home). Charge the stones and "refresh" the visualization on a monthly basis or as you feel it is needed.

·················
Creating a House Guardian
by Edward Rickey

There is a tradition within Western ceremonial magick of creating semi-intelligent entities to carry out the wishes of a magician. Some call these golems or egregores, but in our case we will be using the technique to create a guardian to protect an area, specifically one's home or living space. This idea is slightly modified from the original in Donald Michael Kraig's book *Modern Magick*.

The first thing to do is clearly define what you want this creature to do. In my case, I lived in a very bad neighborhood, with drug dealers, prostitution, and break-ins, but it was the only place I could afford at the time. What I needed was a guard dog of sorts, but I couldn't afford to buy and keep an actual dog where I lived. So I created a guardian to fill the job.

Find or make a talisman to house your guardian. It will be the focal point from which the guardian will operate, its physical anchor to the world and the place it will go when it is not active. I made a dream catcher and added some decorations to it that signified the characteristics the guardian will have. Try a shark tooth, stones like tiger's eye, and so on. These help build up the abilities of the guardian.

The next part is to place the talisman in the area you'd like to protect. I determined the weakest place was the front door, so I hung it on the wall near the door, which is also a place I see every day in order to connect with the guardian. Yours might be a window, bedroom, or living area. The choice will depend on your specific environment and the threat you think is most likely.

Having done this, now comes the actual magic. You will need to visualize this guardian. Is it two legged or four? Does it have fur, scales, feathers, claws, teeth? All these things you need to choose, but don't choose something so hideous or scary that it would frighten you or your guests if they actually saw it. More than once my particular guardian has been seen by others. If you have trouble visualizing this, trust that if your ability to visualize were stronger, you'd actually see it, and know that it is real even if you have trouble seeing it in your mind's eye.

Your guardian should have the intelligence of a dog or cat or some other pet. Not too smart to become dangerous, but smart enough to do its job and make decisions.

Now, give it a name, a simple name that only you know and will always use to refer to it. Let it know that you are its parent, its pack leader, its creator, and the one who will feed it. Let it know that it is the guardian's job to protect the home, the lair for both of you, any who live there, and any invited guests. Anyone else not permitted is to be chased away.

Now let it do its job. In your mind, greet it every day as you would a pet and say goodbye as you leave. Treat it as a living being and communicate with it. Does it have needs? Wants? The more you commune with your guardian, the better your rapport with the being you have created will be, and the easier it will be for you to work with it. Feed it magical energy regularly. The kind of energy should be the same energy that martial artists call *chi* or *ki*, and giving it to your guardian should not deplete you. Direct it to the guardian or to the talisman, whichever is easier.

Should it become necessary to undo the guardian, remember that you created it and you can undo it. Reverse the process of creation. Visualize removing its features one by one and slowly absorb those parts back into yourself. Then, disassemble the talisman, thanking the guardian for its loyal service.

Remember, this is a servant to you, so use it wisely.

On-the-Go Ward

For this ward you will need to create a sigil or bind rune that you will use as your trigger to activate your ward. Instead of hanging fuzzy dice in your car, you can hang your ward from the rearview mirror. Alternatively, the ward could be kept in the glove compartment or another area of the car. Just be certain it does not obstruct your ability to drive safely. Your ward can be as Witchy or mundane as you like. The current ward in my car is a crow feather on a string with some decorations, but for a long time I used a small stuffed Grumpy Cat toy that a store had been selling to hang in a car. It worked just fine despite its mundane appearance.

The bind rune or sigil should be something personal that you create specifically for the purpose of your protection while traveling. It doesn't have to be complex, just have meaning to you.

Hold your item and see it infused with a white light and your will. See a sphere of protection circling your car, sending bad drivers away from you, and keeping you safe on the road. I like to add a layer of thorns just behind that sphere, sending anyone who might take or mess with things that are not theirs far away. When that image is clear in your mind, draw the bind rune in the air over the item. Say these or similar words:

I am safe and I am protected

When you get in the car, draw the rune in the air or see it in your mind to add energy and activate the ward. This can be done every time you drive the car or whenever you feel it is needed.

Cursing

Cursing, with the assumption that we have good reasons to do so, includes ridding yourself of a problem person, breaking a curse directed at you, and calling for justice to be done for a person's wrongful actions. As we are looking specifically at the defensive side of cursing, the following spells can be used as a means of magickal self-defense.

....
Modern Version of a Curse Tablet

Curse tablets can be found in the archeological record throughout the Greco-Roman world. Numerous examples have been found at the temple of Sulis Minerva in Bath in England, and almost a hundred curse tablets were discovered in a nearby temple dedicated to Mercury at West Hill, Uley. Curse tablets sometimes only had the name of the person being cursed along with some descriptive things the curser wished would happen to their enemy. Many called on certain gods to assist in the delivery of the curse. In most cases the tablet was made of soft metal, rolled up, and either buried in the ground, left in a temple (in some cases being nailed to temple walls), or put in bodies of water. Lead was popularly used, although there are examples of curse tablets from Egypt that were written on clay and either smashed or buried. These tablets were sometimes used to give the dead rest or final peace, especially for those who met violent, disquieting ends. When placed at gravesites, they usually petitioned the gods to punish the person who was guilty of causing the deceased person's death.[2]

   For this spell, you will need a sheet of thin metal and a pencil. For modern purposes, you could go down to your local hardware or building supply store and purchase lead sheets. Lead is toxic if ingested or inhaled, and the poisonous quality of it does make sense if you want someone's shenanigans or bad behavior to stop. Although if you plan on disposing of your tablet by leaving it in a body of water, lead is not the best idea be-

---

2. John Gager, *Curse Tablets and Binding Spells from the Ancient World* (New York: Oxford University Press, 1992), p. 19.

cause it can contaminate the water. Using lead in a bottle spell (see page 34) can be quite effective though. If you do choose to use the material, wash your hands thoroughly after handling it and keep it away from pets and children. Thin sheets of steel, tin, or another metal are just as effective and easily purchased at hardware stores.

Although pencils no longer contain lead for obvious safety reasons, I still like using them to write on my tablets for the aesthetics, but you can use whatever medium you prefer to write with.

Cut the metal so that it is about one to two inches wide and three to five inches long. It should be big enough for you to write on without running out of room. You do not have to write a great deal on the tablet—just the basics. The assumption here is that you have a good reason for asking that a person cease harassing you or be sent away so they will no longer harm or trouble you or others. This also means you accept the consequences of the exertion of your will. Banishing someone, stopping someone from doing you harm, and cursing in general don't fall under the category of harm none in my mind. It is exerting your will to obtain a result, a result that can be messy for the person it is being directed at. That is something you need to be comfortable with.

Before writing on your tablet, invoke the deity you wish to aid you in your work. Pour an offering of wine or other spirits, and then praise the deity for the qualities you wish to help you in your working. For example, if I were calling on Badb, I might say,

> *Badb, Battle Crow, you who strike fear into the hearts of the wicked*
> *I call to you to witness and aid in my work*

If I were petitioning Ereshkigal, I might say,

> *Ereshkigal, mistress of the underworld, you who judge the dead*
> *lay down your judgment here, bring justice, and aid my work*

Next, take your tablet in your hands. You can use the following as an example of what you might write on your tablet:

> (Name of deity), *I petition you to* (curse, bring justice, bring retribution)
> *onto* (name of person)

If you like, you can include a reason or a description of the outcome you wish to occur. Hold the tablet in your hands and see the outcome you desire coming to pass. Your visualization and the energy you put behind your will in this is what is important. When you are done, pour another offering to the deity you are calling upon to help you complete your task. Bury the tablet away from your property, preferably at a crossroads, or throw it in a body of water.

·················
War Water Curse Bottle

War water is essentially iron rust suspended in water with other ingredients, which can vary depending on the person creating it. Sometimes called Mars water, it is most likely a European contribution to Hoodoo but no less effective. Mars, besides being connected to war, was also connected to iron. Instead of leaving the war water in the vicinity of the person troubling you, you can use a curse tablet as a proxy for that person and place it in the war water.

You Will Need:
½ cup hibiscus flowers
Water
Mason jar
Old nails
½ cup vinegar
Urine
1 egg white
Handful of Spanish moss
Curse tablet (see page 32)

First, steep the hibiscus in 1 cup hot water. You can use more water depending on the size of the jar you are using. An old mason or canning jar will do. Pour the water in the jar and add the rusty nails. Add ½ cup vinegar and the urine. Urine can be used in spell bottles to mark one's territory and for getting someone to back off and stop bothering you. It doesn't have to be a large amount; a small amount is fine. Add the egg white and Spanish moss. Spanish moss grows on trees in the South. It rots especially well in water, giving the water a swampy look and smell, and has become a common ingredient in some versions of war water. Alternatively, you could use old leaves, swamp water, or whatever kind of moss grows locally to you.

As discussed in the curse tablet instructions, lead should be handled with care. Due to its toxic nature, if I do use it, I put it in a bottle spell. Bottle spells can be used for banishing people or getting them to stop bothering you. Use the spell on page 32 to create your curse tablet, and then put it in the jar instead of burying it.

Bury the jar away from your property.

....

Turning Another's Power against Them Spell

by Edward Rickey

The theory behind this spell is the idea that anyone casting a curse or harmful magick creates a link for the magic to flow. That link, like a wire or cable between the caster and victim, can be used cleverly to siphon off the magical energy from the source. That energy is turned away from causing you harm and can be redirected back toward the source, used for other magic, or stored away to charge your later magical workings.

You Will Need:

About 2 feet (60 centimeters) of natural cordage, twine, or string

Bowl of water and a towel to place under it

Scissors or a knife

Convenient container

Begin by creating whatever magical workspace fits with your tradition and experience. The actual construction of the workspace must fit your needs and provide you a space to work in undistracted. Turn off all distractions, such as phones, computers, and televisions.

Next, tie the ends of the string together to make a loop that you can grasp and pull through your hands, like you're reeling in a cord, wire, or fishing line. You should be moving the cord like you're pulling something toward you in one continuous motion. Enough of the cord should dangle down that you can drag it through the water bowl.

When ready, place the loop in your hands with the bottom dangling in the water, so as you rotate the loop around, the top moves toward you and the bottom drags through the water, cleaning it.

Begin moving the loop, seeing the connection between you and the other party as a magical cord, glowing and electric. This is the energy that person is sending toward you, and in your hands is the wire it's traveling on. Begin to pull the cord as if you are pulling the energy toward your hands and chant,

When you push, I shall pull
Where you strike, I will move away, drawing you deeper in to my grasp
Your power is mine to move as my own
Water cleanses it; now it is mine

As the cord passes through the water, really see the water washing away the negative intent and just leaving the string as a crackling live wire of magical energy. See the energy pulled from the source into the loop, and when the time is right, cut the cord, saying,

And now I cut myself free!

The cord may now be used to effect whatever magic you want, saved for a later time, or burned as you see fit.

Flush It Down the Drain Curse Breaking

If you need to break a curse, the obvious question is, how do you tell if some nasty energy has been sent your way? Before you do a curse breaking, it is a good idea to do some divination about the situation. If you are sensitive to energy, you may just get a nagging feeling that something isn't right or there are just too many odd, disastrous coincidences that seem to be happening to you. Another way to see if someone has been messing with you is to do some journey work. Sit quietly and see a thread of energy in front of you. Imagine the thread represents the problems or bad feelings you have been experiencing. You pull on it like a string, and then, with it in your hands, you follow it to the other person it is connected to. Magick, even a curse, is energy, and when someone sends something nasty (or nice, for that matter) our way, it connects us to their energy. Usually, if you follow this thread of energy to its source, you can get a good idea of who the problem person is. But does that mean that person cursed you? Maybe, maybe not. Sometimes even nonmagickal people who have very strong wills that can effectively send negative crap into our lives. Regardless, this spell will send back harmful energy to whoever has sent it.

You Will Need:
Water
Bowl
Salt
Small cloth or face towel
Finger pricker

Pour the water in the bowl, add a few pinches of salt, and stir it in with your finger. Call on whichever deity you wish to work with to do this work, and ask them to bless the water for you. Then, take the wash cloth, dip it in the water, and run the damp cloth over your forehead, arms, and feet, seeing all negative energy attached to you washing away and dissolving. Then take the finger pricker, prick your finger, and let a few drops of blood go into the remaining water. Say,

Blood for blood
What was sent to me I send right back
I wash away its influence
I send it down the drain
Let it return from whence it came
May the evil they have sent me infest them like a plague
May their own evil fill them
I close the door and slam it shut
No harm can come to me
The way is barred forever more

Stir the water with your finger in a counterclockwise motion. See the energy spiraling away from you as if it is being flushed down a drain. See it returning to whoever sent it to you and spiraling back into them. I visualize it going into their solar plexus. This energy was born from them and sticks to them like glue; it's their own mess to clean up, not yours. You are just sending it back.

When you are done, flush the water down the drain or dispose of it off your property. Thank the deity you called on and leave offerings. Also listen for any advice they may give you about protecting yourself in the future.

THE PROCESS OF TRANSFORMATION

Although the term "dark goddesss" is a modern one, the common thread between the gods we give this label to remains the same. They are beings who instigate and navigate us through change. They use destruction as a catalyst. They are liminal deities and the teachers of hard truths. Whether they are helping us change something about ourselves or leading us through the greatest process of change, death, these deities all rule over transformation of some kind. And in order to truly understand them, we must understand the process of transformation itself.

As painful as it is to have some things in our lives torn down, sometimes it really is for our own good. It's human nature to hold on to things for too long, to cling to the things we know even if they are poisonous to our very being. For the most part, we don't like change. And the unknown terrifies us, because there are no guarantees. When we meet dark and dangerous gods, there are no guarantees who we will be at the end of our journey through the dark.

Quite a lot of people find Paganism out of a desire to create real and meaningful change in their lives. The idea of casting spells, connecting to powerful gods, and reshaping our lives into something better than it is can be a tantalizing thought. If I do just the right spell, say just the right chant, I can land the job of my dreams, find love, and have a happy and content life. Magick can do that. The gods can do that. But like any genie worth his salt, they will remind you that wishing for things and, more importantly, manifesting them isn't as simple as you'd like it to be. What we want is the Emeril Lagasse approach to magick. *Bam*, and you got instant change! But it doesn't work that way. There is always, always a price. And we don't like the idea of magick or working with the gods having a price. But trust me, it does. Real magick, real devotion and dedication to deity, has a cost. And it's completely worth paying.

When I am discussing my work with the dark goddess, one of the questions I am often asked is how exactly to go about causing life-changing transformation without causing any harm. The answer is simple and completely not what the person wants to hear: it's impossible, because the concept of harm none doesn't work. When we are "baby Pagans," we buy into the idea that transformation can be as easy as burning a candle and calling on the right kind of god that we find off a list of correspondences on the Internet. Change is a beautiful pain-free process, like a caterpillar morphing into a beautiful butterfly. Love and light. Harm ye none. These are all the lies those new to Paganism are fed, and the old hats fall victim too. So, for the record, change sucks. It hurts. It's painful. And worst of all, there are no guarantees where you will end up when you start down the path of true change, spiritual or otherwise, in your life.

In Paganism at large we get caught up in the idea of the rede, in the idea that to be a Witch you have to work in a "love and light" paradigm. But it doesn't work. It isn't realistic. And not subscribing to these ideas doesn't make you immoral or a bad person. There are many words I use to describe myself. I am a Pagan: I'm a polytheist and see the gods as very real beings with personalities and individual likes and dislikes. I am a priestess: I am dedicated to the Morrigan, and my devotion to her influences and drives much of my work and spiritual practice. And I am a Witch, but I don't buy into the rede. Don't get me wrong—it's a pretty thought. But just by living and breathing, we affect the rest of the world, sometimes in a good, creative way and sometimes in a destructive way. We destroy things to fuel our continued existence on a myriad of levels. The nature that Pagans worship is brutal and deadly at times. Lions eat zebras, and I have no problem seeing this brutal truth as being balanced and having a kind of beauty. Nothing comes for free, especially in magick. And when we get caught up in the idea that we can do magick without a cost, create change without consequences, we are either left wondering why our magick didn't work or why our world is suddenly turning into shit. By "cost" I mean that deep and powerful magick, or deep and powerful transformation, requires work. You don't have to offer a grand sacrifice or your firstborn child to the gods, but the things you want to bring into your life may cost you some tears and some honest soul-searching. Doing the work is a kind of offering to the gods. Scholar and author Morgan Daimler explains,

> There is risk with all-powerful magic, and the bigger and more badass the better the chance that someone's gonna get hurt during the process, and that means the person doing it and that means the people affected by it. When you're trying to shift years' worth of entropy and BS out of your life, you're going to bleed in the process, and you're going to spill blood as well. Some healing can't begin without first opening wounds, and some freedom can't be gained without first cutting away that which holds us back, even if it means cutting out a part of ourselves we don't want to let go of. You can't uproot a tree and replant it without breaking the roots and letting the sap run, after all. If you seek to do such a thing without harm, you have failed before you've begun.[3]

Dark deities will help you through the process of change. They will give you exactly what you asked for but at the same time they expect you to earn it. They will sit there tapping their feet, arms folded over, until you get the point. And that requires a certain amount of trust in the deity. Many people who experience this will chalk it up to the deity being spiteful or dangerous. But they are there to help you work through your darkest fears, your biggest challenges. They are like drill sergeants preparing you for war, for the hard realities of life. They are on your side, but they won't do the work for you.

Perhaps one of the best descriptions I have come across to describe what exactly "change" is comes from a workshop taught by Kirk White at Harvest Gathering several years ago. He was describing how his life changed as he worked through the different levels of initiation within a particular magickal tradition. At one point he commented, "Real change feels like death." And it's true. At its core change is a process of destroying in order to move forward or re-create ourselves or a part of our life. By its very nature, it demands that part of us die or be destroyed to accomplish this. It is a process no more peaceful than a construction crew taking a wrecking ball to an old building to clear the way for a new one is. When governments change, it is often through revolution, warfare,

---

3. Morgan Daimler, e-mail message to author, January 27, 2016.

and violence. When we go through the process of change, at the innermost parts of our being, it is no less violent or chaotic. Nothing in this universe can be created without destroying something in its stead. And breaking down the things that dwell at the core of our being—the things that weigh our spirits down, that can be the hardest to let go of, the hardest to destroy—is not easy, nor should it be. Nor does it happen all at once.

The problem most of us encounter is that the world around us doesn't really want us to change. And as a consequence, we really don't know how to deal very well with change when it does occur or become a necessity. Our culture encourages stability. Change is viewed as a weakness, as a mark of instability and failure. As a child you most likely were asked what you wanted to be when you grew up. Maybe it was a firefighter, a teacher, or a musician. Whatever the answer you gave, there was a certain expectation that you would spend your childhood growing, changing, dreaming, and figuring yourself out. We'll go through angsty teenage years, changing and evolving both physically and mentally, but then at a certain point we are supposed to have figured it all out. That process of change and becoming, we are told, is supposed to stop. Become the firefighter or teacher. Become stable and consistent. Have the steady job or career, the spouse, the 2.5 children. Pay the bills. Live a life of quiet repetition. And once we reach that goal, we are supposed to stay there. Our time for change and evolution reached its conclusion in our youth.

Yet life isn't stagnant, no matter how much we want it to be. We are constantly changing and growing throughout life. In fact the entire point of living is to grow and change. And that requires us to accept that there will be things about ourselves, people, and ideas along the way that we will have to let go of. There is no such thing as happily ever after, because we are constantly growing and changing. More than likely who you were five years ago is not the same person you are now, nor will you be the same five years in the future. The changes aren't always dramatic, but they are there nonetheless.

The more we understand about the process of change, the better equipped we are to journey into the realms of these gods. No matter the situation, whether a physical change or an inner one, in general the steps we take toward transformation are the same. It is a journey that we can find models for in some familiar places. We will be looking at four models in particular, although they are certainly not the only ones that exist. Each model looks at the same problem, how humans deal with change, but tackle and describe the process through different lenses. Elisabeth Kübler-Ross, a psychiatrist, looks at the process through the lens of the medical profession. Friedrich Nietzsche's metamorphoses of the spirit show us change through the viewpoint of philosophy. Joseph Campbell's hero's journey brings us the perspective of the mythologist. Finally, the concept of the descent brings us back to the actual myths themselves. Each describes the same process in different ways, through different filters, to give us a better understanding of transformation. One is not necessarily better than the other, but each describes a universal truth about the process of change.

Kübler-Ross Model of Grief

If real change does in fact feel like death, then it only makes sense to look at the stages of grief in our journey to understand change. The five stages of grief were first introduced by Swiss psychiatrist Elisabeth Kübler-Ross in her book *On Death and Dying*, based on her work with terminally ill patients. Although initially used in reference to her patients' own physical death, Kübler-Ross later expanded this model to include other forms of loss, such as the death of a loved one, chronic illness, losing a job, ending a relationship, and dealing with drug addiction.

Kübler-Ross's stages describe the process we undergo when we are integrating new ideas or information into our reality when those ideas conflict with our previous beliefs. It describes how we come to grips with change and ultimately accept and integrate it into our lives. She notes that some people will experience a roller coaster of going back and forth through the different stages and that not everyone experiencing grief of any kind will necessarily experience all five emotional stages.

Denial

This is the very first reaction to grief or loss. In this stage individuals hold on to the hope that a diagnosis or fundamental issue is a mistake or somehow not true. In the case of a disease the patient believes the test results are somehow false, a child dealing with the separation of his or her parents believes they will get remarried, and in an unhealthy relationship we might choose to ignore certain behaviors. There are endless ways we try to convince ourselves that things we are uncomfortable with don't exist.

Anger

In this stage the individual accepts that denial cannot continue. Frustration and anger may be directed at others, especially caregivers or individuals who are in close proximity to the individual. The individual asks questions such as "How could this happen to me?" and "Why me?" and states that "It's not fair!"

Bargaining

In this stage the individual hopes the situation at hand is avoidable or alterable in some way. This could be by initiating a lifestyle change for an extended life or making compromises in situations not involving physical illness.

Depression

In this stage the individual becomes reclusive, silent, and withdrawn. They may refuse to see visitors or interact with people, and they spend the majority of their time mourning or in a sullen state. They question the point of going on with everyday activities: "I'm going to die soon, so what's the point? Why bother with anything?" Individuals may also burden themselves with guilt and regrets in regard to the situation.

Acceptance

In the final stage the individual embraces the reality or inevitability of the situation or tragic event. Those facing illness and their own mortality enter a retrospective and calmer emotional state. This doesn't necessarily equate to happiness but rather acceptance of the situation and being able to react to it. In leaving a relationship you might make plans for the future. Or you may accept the passing of a loved one or make preparations for their passing.

Nietzsche's Metamorphoses of the Spirit

In *Thus Spoke Zarathustra* Friedrich Nietzsche offers us another model for transformation. While his analogy is influenced by his contempt with some aspects of Christianity, his description of the process of transformation holds true to us today.

Nietzsche writes, "Of three metamorphoses of the spirit I tell you: how the spirit becomes a camel; and the camel, a lion; and the lion, finally, a child." [4] The analogy begins with the strong spirit whom he imagines in the guise of a camel. The camel, being very strong, takes pride in the fact that it can carry a great deal of weight. And so the camel bends and loads himself with weight even to the point of exhaustion. The camel bears the weight of its tasks but eventually finds its work unfulfilling and meaningless and finds himself weighted down in a spiritual desert. No longer wishing to bear the weight and no longer finding meaning in the values placed on itself, it transforms into a lion, a spirit that fights against false values in order to find his own place and freedom. Nietzsche calls the lion the no-saying spirit: its role is to deny and make room for new things. In the spiritual desert the lion battles the dragon "Thou Shalt," representing established values and religion. After confronting the dragon, the lion transforms into a child. As the child, the spirit can experience the world anew, live for the moment, and forget the limitations of the past. The child can see things with new eyes, live for itself, and create a new path.

So what does that mean for us today? Nietzsche's analogy has many layers. How many times have we acted as the camel? When have we taken up tasks and burdened ourselves with things that we should not have taken on? Or taken up tasks that were unfulfilling to us because others have told us we should find them meaningful? Eventually, when we are dissatisfied enough with a situation, we rebel against the things that hold us back. We become the lion and begin living for ourselves, but we must battle the obstacles that block our path. When we have battled our monsters in our spiritual desert, we can transform into the child, start on a new path, and see things in a new way.

The Hero's Journey

We find a similar pattern for change in Joseph Campbell's study of comparative mythology. In his *The Hero with a Thousand Faces* Campbell proposes that throughout world mythology there is a "monomyth," a cycle that is repeated in the adventures and journeys of heroes universally within mythology. The journey of the hero through the underworld is one found in all cultures in one form or another, and perhaps it has remained

---

4. Friedrich Nietzsche, *Thus Spoke Zarathustra* (New York: Macmillan, 1896), p. 25.

so prevalent in our imaginations because the process the hero undergoes is one that we also embark on within our lives.

Campbell breaks down the hero's journey into three parts: departure, initiation, and return. In the departure stage the hero experiences a call to adventure, and the hero then resists the call, usually out of fear or doubt. In some cases another character expresses the danger the hero will face. Afterward, the hero meets a mentor, usually one that is magical in some way or has special knowledge. With the aid of the mentor, the hero is able to cross the threshold of the underworld and enter the next stage of initiation.

Initiation is where the process of change occurs. As the hero travels through the underworld, he faces challenges and sometimes temptations until he is faced with the final ordeal. Usually, the hero gains a treasure or special item from facing this ordeal. In the final stage of return, the hero must experience a resurrection. This can be surviving a battle or test that would be fatal to anyone else or coming close to death and surviving before being able to return to the normal world. The hero returns to the ordinary realm with new knowledge and treasures he has claimed from the underworld.

At times the underworld isn't a literal underworld where the hero faces his challenges. It is simply something outside of the ordinary for the hero; it can be a faraway land, the depths of the ocean, or a dream world. Regardless of whatever our own "underworld" is, it is a place out of our comfort zone and represents something outside our everyday experiences and familiar landscapes.

Campbell's hero's journey is a familiar one. It is Odysseus traveling to the underworld for knowledge, Orpheus descending to Hades to rescue his lost love, and Inanna's descent into the land of the dead. Although we most likely are not physically traveling through the underworld, we experience our own hero's journey throughout dark times in our lives. We all have our own personal hells, our own demons to face in our darkest hours, and our own journey toward the world of light and rebirth. Like the hero, we resist change, we may have mentors and spirit guides who help us make the realization that change is inevitable, and we make our descent into the dark through trials and challenges so that we may return with the knowledge of ourselves and begin anew.

Concept of the Descent

We have looked at change through the lens of the scientist, the philosopher, and the mythologist. When we look at change purely through mythology, there is one more pattern that emerges. The descent is something that is part of the human experience and speaks to us on the deepest of levels. We find it in various forms throughout world mythology. It is the story of Inanna's descent into the underworld; it is Persephone's abduction into Hades's realm. At first glance this may seem akin to Campbell's hero's journey, but there is a key difference. Campbell's hero travels to the underworld or a faraway land to receive gifts and discover allies, while the descent is its shadow opposite. When Inanna travels to the land of the dead, she must leave pieces of her finery at each gate. Persephone must relinquish her innocence to become Hades's queen. The descent is not limited to goddesses; heroes like Orpheus, Heracles, and Odysseus all make journeys to the underworld. While the hero acquires things along his journey, the descent is all about relinquishing the symbols of our status, our pride, and our long-held illusions. Katrina Messenger, in her book *Descent,* uses the mythologies of the descent to describe a matrix for change: "Unlike the hero's journey where at each juncture the hero attains gifts, tools, or allies, the descent journey asks us to relinquish our hard won trophies, shatter our deeply held convictions, dissolve our ego-supporting illusions."[5] She explains, "Myths are like a cultural dream—they represent the journey of a people. There are thematic patterns that repeat across different cultures, which means that those patterns are specific to us as a species. Descent myths in particular are greater than human in their content—they illustrate the patterns of life itself."[6]

From my own experiences, I've learned that we must first go through our own hero's journey before we can experience its shadow side in the descent. We must acquire our guides and tools to help us along the way before we are at a place where we can shed our egos and like Inanna stand naked before the throne of the underworld. It's very much like when one first learns magick. We worry about having all the right tools and can't possibly do ritual without a particular athame or incense. Then later on we discover we can perform magick without any of those things.

---

5. Katrina Messenger, *Descent: A Journey for Women* (Lulu.com, 2011), p. 5.

6. Ibid., p. 6.

We experience the descent throughout our process of change. In shedding certain parts of ourselves, we make room for growth and look at things that we once thought important with new eyes.

If we distill the essence of all these models for change, three key elements emerge as universal. There is a descent, a challenge, and a rebirth. The descent is the journey we take to accepting that change must occur. We accept the circumstances at hand, but at first we may resist taking action or accepting the reality of what we must do or face. In Campbell's model this is initiation, the journey the hero takes in order to descend into the underworld. In the concept of descent it is where we shed our illusions and, in letting things go, make room for change to occur within us. For Nietzsche this is the camel, accepting the heavy load of life and taking on more than he should. For Kübler-Ross this is denial and anger, refusing to look at the truth and asking the world, "Why me?"

The challenge phase is where we enact change and face it head-on. We are truly deep in the depths of the underworld and face the truths and shades we find there. In Campbell's journey it is where the hero faces the temptations of the underworld and fights to capture the ultimate prize. Whether this prize is self-actualization or attaining a goal, it is fought for with determination and through facing the obstacles that block our path. We become Nietzsche's lion in the desert, taking on the battle with the dragon. The darker side of the challenge is Kübler-Ross's stage of depression. We may feel like the obstacles in our path are too much to conquer.

The final stage is rebirth, although the last stage in our process of transformation is really a beginning. It is where the real transformation begins. We have fought the great battle and can now transform from the lion to the baby. We can emerge from the underworld, transformed from our experiences and carrying new, precious knowledge. In our descent we stand at the throne of the underworld naked, having shed our ego and illusions, and can finally transform into something new.

No matter what kind of transformation you are considering embarking on, at some point you will go through these stages. Possibly multiple times, until like Campbell's hero you emerge from the darkness transformed. Each part of the process is just as important as the other, and until we have dealt with each stage, we will keep chasing our tails and returning to the same problems without resolving them. Most of the time even us Pagans want a quick fix. Slap some glue, or magickal glue in this case, on a problem and *bam!* Problem gone. Smudging one's house to banish negative energy isn't the same as really putting our feet on a path of true transformation. Smudging and cleansing your house is important, but it isn't going to make your marriage work or truly get rid of feelings of self-loathing or doubt. More than likely, negativity and the fears we hold inside are things that can't be banished but instead must be faced and utterly destroyed if we are to ever truly be free of them. We cannot look at the difficult things in our lives as something to be banished; instead we must embark on a journey to conquer them and understand why they're a part of us in the first place. It's a daunting task. Luckily, we aren't alone on our journey. There are guides along the way who will teach us, challenge us, and ultimately lead us to rebirth.

In the following sections we will explore each stage of the process of change—descent, challenge, and rebirth—as well as the dark goddesses connected to them. I recommend you start from the beginning and work your way through. Each step is vital. If we haven't properly mourned and cleansed with the goddesses who embody the descent, we may not be ready for the ordeals we face when we meet the goddesses who represent challenge. If a particular dark goddess does not appeal to you and you'd rather work with a different one or one from your own tradition for a particular aspect of transformation, I encourage you to rework the exercises or rituals using the deity of your choice. Even if you do not work with every single goddess that embodies one of these stages of transformation, I suggest you at least work with one from each section.

Each chapter begins with a meditation designed to help you connect to that deity. You can read through the meditation and then do your own journey work based on the images provided, or you can record them and play them back when you are ready to connect to that deity. You will also find suggested offerings and ways you can start a devotional practice with that deity as you go through your journey of transformation.

The time you take working through each stage or with which goddess is up to you. For larger goals, or ones where there is a great deal of emotional trauma to sort through, you may want to take a year, working through a section a month. Or for other types of transformation, you may simply want to take three months to work through the entire three-stage journey. Each person's journey will be unique.

Part 2
The Descent

She who walks the floors of hell finds the key
to the gates of her own Heaven buried there like a seed
—Segovia Amil, *Ophelia Wears Black*

Transformation can be thrust upon us unwillingly or it can be a choice, a journey we embark on with enthusiasm or trepidation. Most of the time we concentrate on the big, dramatic parts of transformation, the crisis point when we are in the middle of facing a challenge head-on. But that is only one small part of the process of true change. We forget to look at the reasons we began the journey in the first place. Looking at the reasons we entered the cave of the underworld can be just as vital to facing the many challenges we will find in the underworld's depths. The reasons we are afraid to enter the cave and the things that prevent us from facing change are also imperative to our journey.

The very first step on our path is an old one, one that both goddesses and mortals have taken. To begin the process of transformation, to enter our own personal underworld, we must, like the reluctant hero, face our fears and take those first brave steps into the dark. We must become Persephone, choosing to journey to the realm of the dead each winter, or Inanna, shedding our egos as we descend into the underworld. Those first terrifying steps into the dark require a choice to face our fears and of our own volition begin the process of transformation.

As with most things, the first step is always the hardest. The trouble with change is that even when we need it the most, we resist it. We bargain with ourselves and create illusions, excuses, and reasons why we really don't have to change, or maybe just not right now. We are scared to march down into the dark road that leads to the deepest, most secret parts of ourselves. Really looking at our problems, at ourselves, can be terrifying. This is not necessarily because of what we will see, but what we know we will have to do when we enter our own personal underworld and really take a good look. If we don't look at our problems, then we don't have to fix them.

We are all afraid of something. Whether the monsters are in the physical realm or the ones that lurk in our psyches, fear is a part of human nature. At its most basic biological level, fear exists to keep us alive. And it does a good job. Fear stops us from doing dangerous things, like going too near the high cliff or toward animals with sharp teeth. When we are in a life-or-death situation, it pumps us full of adrenaline, instinct sets in, and we are given a boost of speed and strength to escape whatever is confronting us. Biologically, fear shuts down our brain's higher rational functions. If a saber-toothed tiger is attacking, we don't have time to think through the problem. Our body needs us to react quickly to survive.

The problem with fear is while at its core it's designed to save us from the saber-toothed tiger, it is also paralyzing at times. Fear can be crippling when we let it run out of control or apply it irrationally, because most of the time we aren't being confronted by a saber-toothed tiger. We are afraid of a whole host of nebulous, vague threats. We are afraid of our own mortality, we are afraid to take action, and at times we are simply afraid of being afraid.

Fear paralyzes us. And sometimes it even tricks us. On a purely physical level fear causes an increased heartbeat, pupil dilation, and an adrenaline and cortisol boost that can make us feel like we are moving and doing something even when we are not. In short, people like to spend time worrying about something because the biological stimuli of fear in our bodies makes us feel like we are actively doing something, even when we are just sitting there stewing about a problem. We aren't really thinking clearly or rationally when we are overcome by fear. But more often than not it is when we are in this irrational state of fear that we make many of our life choices.

When working with the dark goddess, it's important to recognize you will be afraid. When we understand our fears and learn to control our reactions to it, we can master this emotion. In this section we will work with dark goddesses who rule over our descent into the underworld. They are the goddesses who help us move past fear, let go of things that hold us back, and mourn the things we have lost and the lost parts of ourselves. They give us the bravery to take those first steps into the dark unknown. The descent is all about removing illusions, releasing fear, and cleansing ourselves so that we may take the next necessary steps toward transformation.

When you begin your journey, your descent into your own personal underworld, there are three things you must keep in mind:

1. The life you had/are living does not work anymore.
2. The process of change will be painful and uncomfortable.
3. There is no guarantee who you will be at the end of the process.

All three of these statements have rather terrifying implications. The first, of course, is that we must acknowledge that change is needed. The second is that it won't be an easy process or without costs. And last, it will change who we are to go on that journey into the dark. Even we won't know who we will be when we emerge after our journey. But without coming to terms with those three facts, we will never find the courage to take those brave steps into the unknown.

5

The Washer at the Ford

ou stand at the shore of a great river. In some places the water rages past; in others it is calm and gentle. This is the river of life, death, and rebirth. In it flows the blood of the ancestors, the blood of all those who have gone before, the blood of birth, and the blood spilt in battle. All life flows through this river. Its water runs through your veins. And you have passed through this water many times before and you will again.

You are not alone in this place. In the center of the river you see a woman. Her skin pale as bone, her hair black as raven feathers. She stands naked in the river. The red waters swirl around her.

You know this is the Washer at the Ford. Of all the Morrigan's faces, she stands out as being very distinct. Once you have seen her, you will never forget her face. She moves like a bird of prey, her hands reach out into the water, and the fingers are long and end in black claws. And she washes and washes. She washes the armor of the fallen and the banners of the brave, and she washes our souls clean.

You meet her eyes, and she begins to wade through the river to where you stand on the shore. She stops a few feet from the shore, still knee-deep in the red water. She motions you forward with a hand and you take one ginger step into the river, and then more confidently you wade deeper and deeper until you stand before her. The water rushes past your knees and you feel the weight to it, the weight of the life in this water—it is life and death and rebirth. In this water is the potential of all things; it washes away the old and brings new form to all things. Its current is unending, as impossible to stop as the rising and setting of the sun.

The Washerwoman looks at you, considering, and then speaks: "To stand before me you must lay yourself bare, as I come before you. Sovereignty is earned. You have to choose to lay the past *behind you, to leave behind that which no longer serves you. Strive to be worthy. You cannot fool me, for I see your heart."*

She reaches down and scoops up water, pouring it over your head handful by handful. You taste copper and iron. And then she lets her claws rake down your skin as the water flows, until she begins to rip pieces of your flesh away.

"Let it go ..." It is said more as a demand than an encouragement. "No more. I will take it from you; I will rip it away, cut out the rot. Your choice. Let it go, let me do my work, or resist and make it more painful for yourself. I will have my pound of flesh no matter what."

And those claws tear you apart. They rip out all the things that do not serve you, all the things you fear to let go of, all the things you have outgrown, until your chest is hollow and bones protrude from a peacefully empty cavity. And then the rest follows, until you are nothing. You are nothing but pieces when you fall backward into the river. And as you do you feel all that life, all those beginnings and endings, swirling around you. You feel free, because there is nothing but yourself left, nothing but the core of who and what you are. No expectations, duties, others to attend to, only the shining of your own heart. In the river there is nothing but that. And slowly you feel yourself begin to reform. Little bits and pieces around the spark that is the essence of your being, the spark that belongs only to you. And you rise out of the river gasping, blood dripping down your body.

The Washerwoman looks at you and kisses your forehead. "My child, become whole again. Become who you are meant to be. Claim the sovereignty you have handed over to others. If you would pass through the river of life and death, if you would descend into the underworld and return again, then you must know your own worth. You are the child of a queen. Stand tall and be proud."

You take a deep breath and the scene begins to fade, but you know if you ever need to release your sorrows and be cleansed, you can find your way back to the river and the Washer at the Ford.

Badb in her guise as the Washer at the Ford can be terrifying. When I have encountered her, she is at times shrouded, her hands blackened, fingers long like the claws of a bird. Other times she is pale, white as bone from her clothes to her skin and hair. She has the uncanny, and at times uncomfortable, ability to see right through you. The Washer at the Ford sees all the things we hide from ourselves with striking clarity. She will hold you fast with those clawed hands and make you take a long hard look into yourself, but she will mourn with you too. The moments when you cry your heart out, when hope seems impossible, she will stand beside you. She will wail, cry, and mourn with you, but she will also wash away your sorrows and help you move forward.

The Washer at the Ford has gone through a transformation of her own through time. "The Washer at the Ford" is a title given to the goddess Badb, one of the three sisters who form the Morrigan. In this guise she would appear along river fords, washing the clothes or armor of those destined to fall in battle, warning them of their fate. In later times she turned into the banshee and the faery *bean-nighe,* diminishing in status from a goddess to a faery woman washing her bloody laundry by river fords and connected to prophecy, usually concerning death omens.

As a goddess, Badb appears in many forms through Irish mythology. In her war aspect she is *Catha Badb*, literally meaning "battle crow" in Irish, and was said to fly over battlefields, her shrieks inspiring battle frenzy in her favored warriors and madness in their enemies. In the battle of Clontarf in 1014 CE Badb was said to have appeared shrieking over the battlefield, and in 870 CE she was said to appear to incite the armies' battle frenzy.[7] In the *Táin Bó Cuailnge* and the *Cath Maige Tuired* she is a figure that incites battle and provokes heroes.

Although her connection to battle and death is clear, what is the most striking about Badb is her connection to prophecy. Of all the Morrigan's guises it is Badb who repeatedly appears to offer prophecy and warn heroes and gods of what will befall them if they do not change the course of their path. She appears to Queen Maeve in a dream, bringing the news that her son will fall in battle and she must arise to avenge him. In *Tochmarc Ferbe (The Courtship of Ferb)* she is described as a young woman, a "white lady, fair with brilliancy."[8]

In the *Cath Maige Tuired* after the Irish gods have defeated their enemies, Badb is asked what she sees: "Then after the battle was won and the slaughter had been cleaned

7. Daithi O'Hogain, *The Sacred Isle: Pre-Christian Religions in Ireland* (Suffolk: Boydell Brewer Ltd, 1999), p. 66.

8. Arthur Herbert Leahy, trans., *The Courtship of Ferb: An Old Irish Romance Transcribed in the Twelfth Century into the Book of Leinster* (London: David Nutt, 1902. Facsimile by BiblioLife, 2009), p. 78.

away, the Morrigan … proceeded to announce the battle…. And that is the reason Badb still relates great deeds. 'Have you any news?' everyone asked her then."[9] She responds by delivering a prophecy foretelling peace followed by troubling times.

In *Togail Bruidne Dá Derga* Badb appears to a king who had broken all but one of his *geis* (magical taboos usually placed on a hero or king by a goddess). After tricking him into breaking his final taboo, essentially proving his unworthiness to rule, he asks her if she possesses the gift of prophecy, and if so, what does she see? She replies that he will not leave the hostel, except for what pieces of his flesh the crows carry away. Her prediction of his death proves true, as he dies the next day. This kind of death prophecy also follows through in her dealing with the hero Cúchulain. As Cúchulain traveled to what would be his final battle, Badb appears to him and the druid Cathbad as the Washer at the Ford, predicting his death: "'Do you see, Little Hound,' asked Cathbad, 'Badb's daughter yonder, washing your spoils and armor? Mournfully, ever-sorrowfully she executes and tells of your fall, when she signifies your defeat before Medb's great host.'"[10]

In faery lore we find a whole host of faery washers at the ford connected to prophecy, most likely inspired by Badb and her habit of washing bloody armor at river fords. If you approached them with kindness, at times these faeries would grant you a wish. Other times they drowned those who ventured too near.

Mourning

What strikes most people about Badb as the Washer at the Ford is that while she can at times be quite terrifying, when we approach her with an honest desire to release our burdens, she can be quite comforting. She allows us to release pain and trauma; her waters wash away the blood and renew us so that we may fight on.

If you are starting down the path of transformation, chances are there was some kind of catalyst that brought you here. A painful event or realization, or just a vague feeling of dissatisfaction and unhappiness. Or perhaps you know you have to start down the path but don't want to face the things you need to confront in order to change.

---

9. Elizabeth Gray, *Cath Maige Tuired: Second Battle of Mag Tuired* (Dublin: Irish Texts Society, 1983), p. 71.

10. Angelique-Gulermovich Epstein, *War Goddess: The Morrigan and Her Germano-Celtic Counterparts* (Los Angeles: University of California Press, 1998), p. 141.

Before we can start down the path that leads into the underworld, it's vital that we understand why we are taking the journey in the first place. When I was confronted by the Washerwoman and knew I had to end a long-term relationship that had become unhealthy and dissatisfying, it was her capacity to mourn with me that struck me. There were so many things I had to let go of and release into her waters. I had to mourn the loss of the people both he and I were ten years ago and accept we were different people now. I had to mourn a future I thought I could have and the sense that I knew the direction my life was heading. Without fully feeling and mourning these things and accepting them for what they were, I'm not sure I could have taken the next step.

Mourning is an essential part of change; we need that opportunity to grieve, to rage and shriek anger and sadness, to release those feelings before we can do the work that is to come. We are always changing. Sometimes it happens slowly. Sometimes it is quick and cutting. A tragic event changes us, a difficult situation teaches us something about ourselves we never realized, or it's a slow change, almost unnoticeable, but then we stop and realize the person we once were is gone. Think about how you changed from kindergarten to high school, from high school through college or your early twenties, from your twenties to your thirties, and so on. Think about the major events that have shaped you, including those that are more recent. How have you changed? What parts of you are gone? What parts are you trying to cling to that are really no more? Write them down. This can be a list or a paragraph written out, whatever you like.

Spend the next few days or as long as you like mourning the person you were. It can be something simple. A few moments of silence and recognition in front of your altar will do. Decide what the best way of doing this is for yourself and go with what feels right.

Devotional Work and Offerings for Badb

Let me first say that gods can get pissed with you. It happens, trust me. Even through your best intentions, things can get messy or go sideways on you. Badb has certainly helped reshape my life, but there have also been times when I have made a few missteps. Once such case was a public ritual in her honor. The ritual was sound on paper but in practice quickly spiraled out of control. A few people didn't fully understand what they were going to do in the ritual, and another accidently in the heat of the moment called on an aspect of her that we had not anticipated drawing in. In the end it was a mess, and I cut the ritual short, wrapping up in the best way I could in a bad situation. The next day all hell seemed to break loose; people's energies were off, one person's protective talisman disappeared, and another felt someone running fingers through her hair in the middle of the night when no one was there. We also noted that usually in all our other previous rituals, one of the priestesses involved had been cut, by accident and blaming it on clumsiness, and offered the blood to Badb on the day of the ritual. That had not happened this time. The day after the ritual everyone in the ritual went back to the ritual area and left offerings in the river that stood nearby. And a few of us specifically left offerings of our own blood.

Since that experience, offering blood has been a regular part of my devotional work to Badb. Blood offerings have a kind of stigma, and some view it as taboo. Using blood as an offering differs from both blood sacrifice and blood magick, although using blood for either of those purposes has been stigmatized as well.

If you do choose to offer blood as an offering, whether to Badb or another deity, before you go running to sharpen your athame, there are some considerations to keep in mind. For safety reasons I personally prefer to use a lancing device. These can easily be found in the diabetic supply section of any pharmacy. While I have used a knife in the past, most of the time a ritual blade or pocket knife is not sanitary, nor is it sharp enough to easily pierce skin. Using a dull or semisharp knife can be more dangerous than using a razor-sharp one. If you have to really push hard to cut yourself, you are more likely to do more damage to yourself, cut too deeply, or cut a vital place you don't want to cut. A lancet is safe, sanitary, and disposable. Offering a few drops suffices for my own practices; you really shouldn't need to offer more than that.

Another safety concern to keep in mind is your comfort level with piercing your skin. If you are not comfortable with this idea or if you have had any issues that involve self-harm, you should not be engaging in this kind of offering. There are plenty of other things to offer.

Before offering blood, I spend a few moments thinking about the reason I am making the offering. My blood carries my life force, my essence, and that is what I am offering to the deity in question. I am offering a very personal part of myself to them, in service, as gratitude. There is also the element that I understand that things have a cost, sometimes a painful one. And making this kind of offering is a way for me to express that I understand that cost.

Another more intense way to offer blood would be by getting a tattoo. This is obviously something you probably are not going to do very often though. The pieces I have are devotional pieces for certain deities. Before going under the needle, I leave an offering at their altar and offer both the pain and blood of the experience to the deity in question.

....

Leaving a Blood Offering to Badb

This is only an example of one way you could go about leaving a personal offering of this nature. Feel free to alter it or find what works best for you. Again, this is something you should be completely comfortable with. If not, you can easily substitute the line "I offer the essence of myself" with "I offer (whatever it is you are offering instead)" when leaving an offering to Badb.

> *Badb*
> *Battle Crow, Banshee*
> *Washerwoman wailing at the ford*
> *I offer the essence of myself to you*
> *For _____*

If you are not making an offering for a specific purpose, such as "for helping me overcome XYZ battle," you could say "in service to you" or "in gratitude to you."

....

Evocation to Badb

BY KAREN STORMINGER

> *Smoke rises and the darkness falls*
> *Hear the drumbeats pounding, our hearts beating in our tightened chests*
> *We call to you, Badb! Phantom queen!*
> *You enter on rushing wings and breath leaves*
> *The connection is made, concussion, collapsing, gasping!*
> *Fear! No!*
> *Hooded one, you who will not abide an atmosphere filled with weak-kneed trepidation*

We know the choice is always ours to make

Stepping forward, we approach the red-stained waters

White Lady, Washer Woman, Crimson-Taloned Queen!

You who circles 'round, red-rimmed eyes piercing through the darkness

Badb, your clawed hands reach out and anchor our unsteadiness

Each of us makes the choice today to accept your gifts, release our fears, and make an oath to

you, to ourselves

In your presence, breath returns, uncertainty flees, the pain subsides

Badb, we call to you in the darkness, in the flickering firelight!

Badb, we call to you whose wings whisper in the cool, black night!

Badb, we call to you as the blood trickles from your clawed hands

Badb, we stand in the water, pools of ruby liquid

Prophetess, come show us the way!

....

Waters of Badb Cleansing

This is something I do quite often and sometimes use as a type of morning devotional when I wish to connect to Badb. It can be used as a daily cleansing ritual and a way to connect more deeply with Badb and her energies.

In the morning (before a ritual or whenever you choose) anoint yourself with some salt. I usually anoint my brow and my heart. Using salt is not strictly necessary, but I like to use it to add an extra cleansing level. I use salt for cleansing in general and even carry the salt packs you'd find in fast-food restaurants in my purse for times when I need to ground quickly and for those unforeseen magickal emergencies when you need some protection or cleansing. For this cleansing I like to use bath salts that have been mixed with a few drops of essential oils. They tend to have a kind of sticky quality to them and allow the mixture to stick to the skin easily as you anoint yourself. If you choose, you can easily draw a sigil or symbol on your skin with the salt and oil mixture. Alternatively, you can put some table salt in a bowl and add a few drops of water to it, stirring it around to get the same consistency.

Once you have anointed yourself, go into the shower, washing yourself with the salt and whatever else you choose. Alternatively, you can do this in the bathtub if you like, although I like the feeling of the running water of the shower to replicate the sensation of rushing river water. See yourself standing in Badb's river, the river that holds all life. See the waters washing over you. Let them take away the things you wish to cleanse yourself of until you see yourself glowing with light, cleansed and full of energy. Thank Badb or say any words you wish to say to her.

····················

A Ritual of Release

You Will Need:

Large bowl

Water

Cranberry juice or wine (optional)

Pen and pieces of paper

Place a bowl of water on your altar. Hold your hands over it and see it as the river of the Washerwoman. You could even put a few drops of wine or cranberry juice in it to make it red tinged. On a piece of paper write the aspects of your life that you want to let go of, or simply "the parts of me that are no more." If it's more than one thing, tear off each thing as you write it and place the pieces of paper in the bowl of water. Say whatever feels appropriate, in these or other words:

Badb, Lady of Prophecy
Lady of the river of life and death
Red-mouth Badb who weaves the fates of heroes
Washer at the Ford who guards our deaths
I recognize the parts of myself that are gone, that are no more
I mourn
I honor what I have been
And I let it go

When you are done, pour the water outside. Dispose of the paper, or let it dry out and then burn it.

·················
Badb's Ritual Bath

BY ELLIE HEFFERNAN

You Will Need:

1 tablespoon dried juniper berries

1 cup dried hibiscus flowers

1 tablespoon dried mugwort

1 tablespoon dried wormwood

1 gallon purified water

1 tablespoon black salt

¼ cup white salt (or Celtic gray salt)

5 drops sandalwood essential oil

¼ cup lemon juice

I find that bathing can be used as an effective mode of ritual preparation. It is a good chance to shed everything that is not essential to the ritual or anything that is not meant to be brought into sacred space. We enter sacred space as all aspects of our complete selves; however, we also sometimes carry residual energy or heaviness from other stressors in life, other people, and so on. It's important to clear that away before we can fully bring all that we are, and only what we are, to where we must be bare. Bathing can also be relaxing and meditative and help prepare the appropriate headspace for ceremony.

Using a large pot, combine the juniper, hibiscus, mugwort, and wormwood with a gallon of purified water. Bring the herbs to a boil and then remove the brew from the heat. Cover the pot and let the herbs steep until they are warm to the touch. Filter out all of the larger particles. Draw a bath and add the filtered tea, salts, essential oil, and lemon juice. Before bathing, visualize the black river, Badb's healing waters. Hear the stream rushing, smell the aquatics and herbs mingled with otherworldly greenery, and then slowly step into the bath, feeling yourself step into a gurgling river to be cleansed.

·················

Badb's Protective Amulet

by Ellie Heffernan

You Will Need:

1 small wooden disk, about 2 inches in diameter (a disk cut from a thick tree branch and sanded smooth is preferable)

Wood burner, rotary tool, or fine-point permanent black marker

Clear epoxy or hot glue

1 small tumbled jet stone

1 small rough garnet

1 small tumbled smoky quartz

Acrylic art sealant (optional)

On one side of the wooden disk, draw or otherwise inscribe a symbol that you most associate with Badb above the ogham for protection, *luis* (rowan) ⊤⊤ or *ngetal* (broom) ⫛ . Otherwise, a sigil of your own creation would also work if you so desire. Draw a triskele on the other side of the disk and glue the three stones onto the three points of formation. Optionally, seal the wood to make it moisture resistant.

The amulet can be wrapped and strung into a necklace to be worn, or simply keep it on your person or hidden somewhere in your home for protection.

6

Akhilandeshvari

You find yourself on the shores of wide, sprawling river. It is warm, and the sun reflects off the water as it lazily flows by. The sound of the water is calming, and you walk the shore, enjoying the sound and the warmth of the sun.

Soon you come to a sandy embankment where the river has washed up a large amount of silt and fine sand from the riverbed. You wonder if it was perhaps caused by a storm, and as you walk along the area, you soon see there are stones and other objects partially buried in the washed-up silt. One looks familiar to you, though you are unsure how it could have ended up here in this place. On your knees, you use your hands to brush away the dirt and sand. And slowly, the object comes into focus. Take a moment to look at it. It is something precious to you from the past, something you treasure. Perhaps you thought you had discarded it, or perhaps you are so afraid of losing it that you have held it close to you for some time. You hold the object in your hands, remembering why it has value to you.

Behind you there is a sound, splashing in the otherwise quiet river. Startled, you turn around to see a giant crocodile heaving itself out of the river just a few feet from where you kneel in the sand. Frightened, you drop the object and hear it shatter as you scramble to get away from the shore and the gaping maw of teeth that is looking at you with far too much interest. But as soon as it is on the shore, the crocodile turns its head and regards you with a large reptilian eye. It makes no move to attack, but instead seems to be waiting for you to do something. Still paralyzed with fear, you feel unable to move. The crocodile nods its head toward the now-broken object you found and remains in place on the shore. With a little trepidation, you walk slowly back to where the shattered pieces lay in the sand. You look at your treasured item with a sinking heart, pick up a few of the pieces, and attempt to fit the jigsaw back together again.

And then you hear a sound. At first it sounds like a breeze moving through the trees, but then it grows louder and you see a swirling whirlwind of golden light hovering just above the river's water. The crocodile moves back into the water and swims just under the swirling light. A moment later the light solidifies, and you see a woman standing on top of the crocodile. You blink several times as you look at her. Her rich mahogany skin glows with a soft light, but she seems to change position every few seconds; her clothes, her hairstyle, and even the color of her eyes change as well. It is as if the light that makes up her form is constantly changing and rearranging the way the pieces of her form are put together.

She gestures a hand toward the broken treasure you hold, and you find that it is suddenly whole again. You hold it up to inspect it in awe. It is in one piece, yet it is also very apparent where it has been broken. Long lines of gold crisscross the item, as if it were fused together along the broken edges with liquid gold. And somehow that makes it more beautiful.

"Nothing can remain frozen in time forever. You try so hard to prevent change. But the universe is ever moving, ever changing, and it will not let you stand still. You fear being broken, yet you forget it is the only way you can move the pieces of your life into new shapes. You are no different from the item you hold. There is beauty in breaking, only to be remade more splendid again. Only then do we know what we are made of."

She holds her hand out to you, and, unafraid, you take it and step onto the crocodile's back. The crocodile swims farther down the river, and as it navigates through the waters, you feel yourself glowing, the light within burning bright and coming to the surface. And like Akhilandeshvari you find the shape of your form changing, no longer keeping solid. You think of all the things you want to reshape in your life, all the pieces of your soul that need to be reshaped, and in your mind's eye you see these things changing, breaking, and reforming in the glow of your own inner light.

The goddess puts her hands on your shoulders and says softly, "Do not fear change. Every time you feel your life is shattered beyond repair, I will be at your side. I will show you that you can rebuild and be the more beautiful for it." The river begins to fade, and you know that when you feel broken inside, you will be able to call on Akhilandeshvari's light and begin to reshape yourself.

✳ ✴ ✳

Akhilandeshvari is the somewhat obscure Hindu goddess who presides at the temple in Tamil Nadu in southern India.[11] She is connected to the element of water, navigating the river of the universe atop a ferocious crocodile. Known as the "goddess who is never not broken," she is portrayed with her body divided in many floating pieces, not quite whole and not quite shattered either.

What is beautiful about Akhilandeshvari is that the very thing we dread the most is the very source of her power: she is in pieces. She is broken, constantly moving and creating new experiences and wisdom out of the broken pieces. She rides a threatening crocodile, symbolizing our fears, to navigate and propel her forward. She accepts her fears and that we are never complete, that we are instead constantly forming and reforming. We are always broken, and to grow we must be. Akhilandeshvari reminds us that being broken into pieces by disaster, heartache, and trauma is an opportunity to re-create ourselves. She intentionally remains constantly in flux, ever tearing herself apart, creating and re-creating herself. Akhilandeshvari is ever open to change. Resolutely, she refuses to be limited, to be stagnant in a single form.

As much as we wish it were not true, our biggest breakthroughs often involve pain and risk. Routine and stability at times prevent us from growth. We cling to routine because it is familiar, no matter how unhealthy it may be for us. Familiarity is safer in our minds than the unknown. Yet you are at your most powerful when all the comforts of routine have been ripped away from you, when you have no other choice than to pick yourself up and change. That moment when you are broken and bleeding inside, when you are on the floor weeping and shaking. In that moment, no matter how broken you are, you are at your most powerful. There is nothing else left to lose, nothing else to hold you back, and all your potential is at your disposal. In that moment all things are possible and nothing is off the table.

Unlike some of her more fearsome counterparts, who wear severed heads and look horrific, Akhilandeshvari instead is portrayed as calm and peaceful. She may rule over what to many of us represents the most difficult times of upheaval in our lives, but she does so with a kind of serenity. To Akhilandeshvari, failure is not a sin, not something

---

11. Preeity Verma, *Small Changes, Big Difference: 7 Ideas for Personal Transformation* (Gurgaon: Partridge India, 2014), p. 55.

to be looked down upon. She pulls herself apart intentionally, knowing it's her choice how she puts the pieces back together. She teaches us to accept that failure is inevitable, that at times it's needed. We will all fail at something, and when we spend all our time and energy pretending that we have not failed at something or that we can fix it, we rob ourselves of the lessons we can learn from the experience.

In her speech at a Harvard commencement ceremony in 2008 J. K. Rowling described how failure reshaped her life:

> I had failed on an epic scale.... I was the biggest failure I knew.
> ... So why do I talk about the benefits of failure? Simply because failure meant a stripping away of the inessential. I stopped pretending to myself that I was anything other than what I was, and began to direct all my energy into finishing the only work that mattered to me. Had I really succeeded at anything else, I might never have found the determination to succeed.... And so rock bottom became the solid foundation on which I rebuilt my life. [12]

There is a certain kind of shame that comes with failure, in not having our lives "together." Many times we go to great lengths to hide the parts of ourselves that we perceive as broken: an unhappy relationship, an addiction we can't overcome, an event from the past we can't get over. Admitting to others that there are parts of ourselves or our lives that don't work, that we are falling apart, can seem like an admission of failure. But we forget that failure at times is natural. We can't win everything. We can't figure everything out all the time like in a fairy tale. Yet there are things we learn from failure, from being broken, that we can attain no other way. To gain power from being in such a state seems unthinkable. At least it does until we admit that in one way or another we are always broken, that we are many pieces constantly moving and finding how they fit or don't fit together. Our lives and minds move and shift like tectonic plates. If one piece stays static too long, the others shift and push against it till some massive tectonic explosion occurs. If we were one solid piece, if we really had everything figured out, life

---

12. J. K. Rowling, "Text of J.K. Rowling's Speech," *Harvard Gazette*, June 5, 2008, http://news.harvard.edu/gazette/story/2008/06/text-of-j-k-rowling-speech.

would be static, and we would have no capacity to change or learn. And this is Akhilandeshvari's lesson, that failure is not a sin and that at times we need to fail; we need things to fall apart all around us to be able to reshape who we will be.

Spiritual Bypass and Accepting Failure

When working with Akhilandeshvari, it is impossible to not contemplate what failure or being broken really means. We all have had moments in our lives, probably life-changing ones, when we felt like our lives were shattered. Our failures can range from our first broken heart in grade school to the more devastating failure of losing a job or loved one in our adult lives. But regardless of how life-altering or minimal these failures were, more than likely we were ashamed of them. Failure isn't fun, and at the time it's hard to see how it can have a positive effect on our lives. In fact in many ways our modern culture has a bit of an obsession with being positive. With spirituality, we are taught how to rid ourselves of "negative" energy, a term we lump into an ominous box that encompasses all that is bad in our lives and ourselves. But if we are always trying to be positive, we never really open up that box and explore what is inside. We never really deal with it, and there is not enough sage in the world to banish those things we refuse to look at.

Morgan Daimler describes this obsession with being positive and the spiritual concepts of love and light as an imbalance that occurs when we don't explore our darkness. We must, like Akhilandeshvari, see the value in breaking ourselves apart to re-create ourselves from the very foundation. In a *Patheos* post about our shadow, Daimler writes,

> In my experience, many pagans seem to think that positive emotions [equal] success and negative emotions [equal] failure in a spiritual sense. I disagree. Both are part of the human experience. You can't idolize one while demonizing the other or you have created an impossible imbalance....
>
> ...[T]here is a real risk with this mindset that we are creating an idea that if being sad or depressed is failing spiritually people will be even less likely to seek help when they need it for clinical depression and that really worries me; we as a community should be a support for people who need help, not an additional

barrier creating unrealistic expectations of perfect happiness 24/7. Spirituality should make your life better, ultimately, not worse."[13]

At its core, this overemphasis on the positive and demonizing of failure is a kind of spiritual bypass. The term "spiritual bypass" was "first coined by psychologist John Welwood in 1984" to describe "the use of spiritual practices and beliefs to avoid dealing with our painful feelings, unresolved wounds, and developmental needs."[14] Welwood suggested it was a fairly prevalent crutch, regardless of religious preference, that usually becomes noticed only in its most extreme cases.[15] In its most basic sense spiritual bypass is avoidance put into a spiritual context. Robert Augustus Masters, author of *Spiritual Bypassing*, argues that part of the reason for the existence of spiritual bypass is that "we tend not to have very much tolerance, either personally or collectively, for facing, entering, and working through our pain, strongly preferring pain-numbing 'solutions,' regardless of how much suffering such 'remedies' may catalyze."[16] We try to apply the same logic to our spirituality as we do to taking an aspirin to make our headache go away. Within Paganism, negative emotions are things we burn sage to banish and buy crystals to absorb and negate. We talk a lot about how to get rid of negative energy but never really how to deal with it. Or that it can be useful. If we don't face the darker parts of ourselves, the parts of our lives that are broken, then we can never learn from them. We'll spend all our time banishing them and wondering why they keep reappearing.

Our concept of the spiritually enlightened person needs to radically change. Take a minute to really think about a person you think of as enlightened. It can be a person you know, someone famous, or just your own made-up ideal. What does that person look like? What do they act like, how do they appear? Is it a mountain guru who wears a peaceful, detached expression? Or is it maybe a familiar face with strength and resolve

---

13. Morgan Daimler, "Irish-American Witchcraft: The Value of Our Shadow," *Patheos* (blog), February 2, 2016, http://www.patheos.com/blogs/agora/2016/02/irish-american-witchcraft-the-value-of-our-shadow/.

14. Robert Augustus Masters, *Spiritual Bypassing: When Spirituality Disconnects Us from What Really Matters* (Berkeley, CA: North Atlantic Books, 2010), p. 1.

15. Ibid.

16. Ibid.

who has weathered life's storms? There is no right or wrong answer, but it is important to consider what that image looks like to us. Spiritual enlightenment doesn't have to wear the face of the always positive, peaceful guru. It's okay to feel pain and sadness. Those things are part of our spirituality too and shouldn't be swept under the carpet as shameful things that, as we become more spiritually evolved, will no longer be part of our existence or have meaning.

Devotional Work and Offerings for Akhilandeshvari

Devotional work with Akhilandeshvari can consist of meditation and inner work. Forgiving ourselves for failures and seeing the beauty in them and how they have changed our lives and influenced us is a task that takes time and a great deal of looking within. If you are having a moment of doubt or a horrible day, sit in front of Akhilandeshvari's altar and ask her to help you and show you that failure is a part of life. Remember that you are constantly being destroyed and re-created like the goddess herself.

When I first started honoring Akhilandeshvari, I started noticing broken things. I found a small kintsugi bowl that I use for offerings to her. *Kintsugi* is a Japanese art form of repairing broken bowls or other pottery by putting gold in the cracks to fix them, making them beautiful because they are broken. In her bowl I started putting pieces of sea glass and other broken things that I felt still had a beauty to them. At times I would hold some of the pieces while I meditated on how things that had ended or broken down in my life had turned into something beautiful or changed me in a powerful way. When the bowl is full of odds and ends, I try to piece them together in a pleasing way and create some kind of art with them. I might glue them onto a board or decorate an object with them.

How you choose to honor Akhilandeshvari can be as personal or creative as you like. Whatever you do to honor her, allow yourself time for self-reflection.

················

Evocation for Akhilandeshvari
BY KAREN STORMINGER

Broken One, divine in all your pieces
Turning upon a sacred point

I call to you, Akhilandeshvari

Stagnant wholeness does not suit you

Ever changing, ever becoming

Fear will not consume you

Let it not overtake me

Instead you choose to ride upon its back

Embracing loss and brokenness

Teach me to embrace my own loss, to revel in my pieces shattered upon the ground

Gnashing, thrashing

Letting the movement swiftly change you

Splintered pieces washing upon the shore

You gather strength with each shard

Show me how to gather my own strength as I collect the jagged edges of myself

A mosaic of fluid beauty, re-creating yourself, re-creating myself as you do

Swirling, whirling, twirling

Wild dervish of life

Your light seeps through the cracks and

I see deep within myself, my own illumination through you

Beacon of change, strength, growth, and resilience

Akhilandeshvari, you are the beauty of life's ever constant destruction and rebirth

I call to you, Never-Not-Broken One

....

A Ritual to Celebrate Failings

Our failures are usually the things we want to sweep under the rug. They are the things we want to forget or run endlessly through our heads trying to figure out how we could have possibly arrived at another outcome, how we could have done something differently. But our failures shape us. They force us in new directions, and, although painful at the time, when we look back, often we find that they were defining moments in our lives. Where would we be if they had never occurred? How would we be different?

It has become a kind of tradition on Samhain for me to honor the person I used to be. It was part of a ritual the group I work with had done for a Samhain ritual some years ago, and I continue the practice in my own personal work around the holiday. In the ritual we had a moment of silence for everyone to mourn the parts of themselves that were no more, when we could contemplate how we had changed, release the people we were, and welcome the people we were now. This ritual is a kind of follow-up to this idea, celebrating where we failed and how those failures have influenced us as well as allowing ourselves to know that these mistakes were okay, if not painful, to make. Failure is a part of existence. Being broken is a part of life's journey. Being at peace with that painful fact is important. It is the first step to allowing us to forgive ourselves for our failings.

You Will Need:

Modeling dough or any kind of quick-drying clay

White candle or picture of Akhilandeshvari

Towel or newspaper

Offering bowl

Offering of your choice for Akhilandeshvari

Before the ritual, take the dough or quick-drying clay and roll it out so it's a fairly flat piece. You may wish to use a rolling pin or a bottle covered in plastic wrap to do so. Next, find different things that will make interesting patterns. This can be anything from something you find in the craft store to using a fork to make lines and impressions in a pleasing manner in the clay. You could write out words in the clay that represent the things you feel you have failed at or are challenged by. If these things are better represented by symbols, you can carve those into the clay and press small crystals into the clay. Whatever you like. If you are using quick-drying clay, let it dry overnight. Modeling dough may require a few days to dry completely. Otherwise, you can dry it using a hairdryer or bake it in the oven for 5 minutes on the lowest setting to quicken the process.

If you wish to cast a circle or call quarters, do so, but it is not necessary. You may wish to have a picture of Akhilandeshvari or simply use the candle to represent her. Light the candle, saying,

Akhilandeshvari, I call to you
Never-Not-Broken
You who tear yourself apart endlessly
Destroying and reforming

Reshaping, remaking
Akhilandeshvari
May I know your serenity
In the face of change
May I know not fear
May I know your strength
As I reshape my life

Take a few moments to see Akhilandeshvari in your mind's eye. Is she riding on the back of her crocodile? Is she in many hovering, swirling pieces or solid? When you see her clearly and feel her presence, take the clay sheet you have created. Place it on the towel or newspaper so you have a surface that can catch any stray pieces. Hold the clay in your hands and think about every time you feel you have failed, weren't good enough, or were unable to change something that you wanted to turn out differently, or all the trials and hardships you have faced. Feel them going into the clay. When you are ready, drop the clay or slam it down (without hurting your hands) on the towel so that it breaks into many pieces. Say,

I am allowed to fail
I have failed
I will fail again
Before me are the shards of myself
The failures that shape myself
The pain that had helped me remake myself
The scars that are part of my being
I am allowed to fail
I have failed
I will fail again
I will shatter what I am
And be remade anew
I will be like Akhilandeshvari
I will tear myself apart again and again
Ever changing, ever becoming

Pick up one of the broken pieces and look at the patterns on it. By breaking it, you have created something new and unique that didn't exist without having been shattered. Even though it is no longer part of the whole, it still can contain a beautiful pattern. Hold the piece up and name it.

This is _____

Once you have named what failing or painful event you want the piece to represent, think of how it changed you for the better or something good that came out of it.

From it I have gained _____

When you are done, put that piece into the bowl as an offering to Akhilandeshvari. Do this for as many pieces as you feel you need to. If you have extra pieces, you can discard them. When you are ready, leave the other item you have set aside as an offering to Akhilandeshvari. It could be flowers, herbs, milk, or some other item that has meaning to you.

Thank Akhilandeshvari and ask her to allow you to see the blessing failure can have and to honor how these things have shaped you.

You may want to revisit the pieces over the next couple of weeks, take one out of the bowl, and meditate with it for a while before putting it back. When you feel the time is right, thank Akhilandeshvari and discard the pieces in whatever way you feel appropriate.

....
Putting the Pieces Back Together Spell

You Will Need:
Old puzzle
Permanent marker
Candle

For this spell, we will be calling on Akhilandeshvari to help us put the pieces of our lives back together.

There may be no guarantees as we go through the process of transformation, but whether it is the hero or the goddess who makes the journey, they always have a clear mission in mind. Think about what you wish to accomplish or what you want to change. How do you want to reshape your life? Which pieces no longer fit—relationships, behaviors? Is it a habit? An issue from the past holding you back? Whatever it is, really take some time to sit down and write out what you hope to accomplish, what you want to change, and what to the best of your knowledge you want the outcome to look like. This may mean you need to take time to really outline the problem or challenge your views on the problem. You must also consider your ability to achieve the goal. For example, does the goal involve other people? You may have to accept that you can only change your own behavior and that you cannot influence the choices of others.

Now create a mission statement. This should be something short, a sentence or two that clearly defines your goal. Once you have that, the next thing you will need is an old puzzle. You can find them in the kids' aisle in stores or in most dollar stores. Pick one that doesn't have a large number of pieces (between ten and twenty-five is a good range; avoid one with over a hundred tiny pieces you can't write on). If you find a puzzle that has a picture on the front that appeals to you, then you can simply put the puzzle together and use a sharpie and write on the picture side your mission statement. You could also use paints of your choice to paint over the image and either draw something that represents your mission statement or paint it a solid color and then when it dries write out the mission statement with a permanent marker or paint. Once that dries, take the puzzle apart and turn the individual pieces over to the blank side (the opposite side from the one you painted). Use the marker to write one or two words that describe parts of your goal on all the pieces. These should be important "puzzle pieces" that will help you accomplish the goal you wrote out on the front of the puzzle.

When everything is dry, go to your ritual space. Invoke Akhilandeshvari and place the puzzle pieces in a pile before the candle. Light the candle, saying,

Akhilandeshvari, this candle's flame is the force of my will
It burns bright against the obstacles I face
Goddess who is never not broken
Help me to reshape the pieces of my life
Let me forge a new path through the fire of my will
Let me arrange the scattered pieces of my life into a new whole
Akhilandeshvari, aid me in this task!

Move the puzzle pieces around with your hands, and then slowly start putting it together. Look at the word written on the back of each piece. Allow this process to be a quiet meditation, while also holding the image of your final goal in your mind. Once you have put the puzzle together, say,

Akhilandeshvari, I reform and reshape my reality
Help me manifest the change I seek

Thank Akhilandeshvari and leave her an offering. You can leave the puzzle in a safe place or on your altar space until the change has manifested, or you can routinely take it apart and put it back together every so often to add energy to your working.

7

HEKATE

You find yourself encompassed in the pitch black of a great cavern. Although you know you have your eyes open, you can see nothing. You feel a hard stone surface under your feet, jagged and rough, like a cave floor. Reaching out your hands in either direction, you expect to feel stone walls on either side, but they touch nothing but air. Even when you reach above you, the ceiling, for you feel certain you are underground, is distant and unreachable.

Uncertain, you walk carefully through the dark, feeling ahead of you with your bare feet. The cave floor is rough, but you find it even enough to walk comfortably along. You continue on for what feels like a long while, the darkness never breaking. There is no prick of light to indicate there is a way back to the world above. Only endless darkness. No matter how quickly you move through the cave, no matter what direction you move, it feels like you might as well have not moved at all. It occurs to you that you even might have been moving in a circle. Without light there is no way of telling, really. In a moment of despair you sit upon the floor, ready to give up. Then your hands brush up against something on the cavern floor. It makes a metallic sound as your fingers push it accidently across the stone. As you reach out, your fingers close around a large, circular piece of metal. You lift it up and feel the other pieces of metal that hang from it with your other hand. They are keys, large ones, on a metal ring. You feel them in turn, each different from the other. And that's when you see it. It's tiny, but it stands out in the unending darkness: a prick of light far in the distance. It flickers and sways almost like a tiny flame.

Clutching the keys in your hand, you hurriedly move toward it. The flame grows bigger, encouraging you to move faster, and soon you realize it's not one but two flames, torches perhaps. And you realize the light is moving. Although you saw no walls before, now you clearly see a rough-hewn wall of black stone to your right. Whatever the light is, it starts to fade a bit as it begins to round a bend into another section of the cavern. Eagerly you pick up speed, no longer careful of your footfalls, not willing to lose the light.

Rounding the curve in the stone wall, you almost collide with the source of the light. They are in fact two torches. They are long and bronze, their flames emanating brightly, though there is no evident source of fuel. They are held by a woman, one in each hand. At first you had not noticed her at all, though now that you look at her it is impossible to notice anything else. She is quite clearly a woman; you can see the curve of her face framed with dark hair and the folds of the dark-colored robes she wears. But behind all that there is something else. Although you see the woman, another image overlays that reality. You see a black void, and you realize she is the source of the darkness. The void you see, with the vague outline of a woman, pulses and hums with its own kind of life. And you fear if you gaze at it too long it will suck you in, like the crushing gravity of a black hole. The woman speaks, and gladly you concentrate instead on the woman's face and not the black depth behind and beneath her. She is young and ageless all at the same time.

"You seek me, yet you do not know why. You seek my help, yet you turn it away. You have wandered through the dark, thinking you were meant to escape it, when instead you must embrace it."

You look down dubiously at the keys in your hands. There has to be a way out.

"I light the way, but I am the darkness. I am the sin-eater, I am the velvet void that devours, I am annihilation and deliverance. I am the void of space that is the night sky and the depths of the sea, and I stand watch at the heart of the storm within you. The keys unlock the things within you that you have buried away, the choices you refuse to look at. I am the keeper of many doorways, many crossroads, and there is no time left for you. You must choose. You cannot dwell in the dark forever."

And for a moment you no longer stand in the cave but at the gates of a large city. A small nook next to a massive stone entranceway holds a small shrine. In it is a carved image of a woman holding two torches, with candles and offerings laid before the image. Then you find yourself standing at a crossroads, two dirt paths extending into a dark forest with the barest sliver of a moon shining above. Then you find yourself in the cave again, keys still clutched in your hands. You bring them to your chest and clutch them close, thinking of the things you fear to choose, the choices you wish you could avoid making.

"I am Hekate, I am the sin-eater, I am the darkness, and I am the light that guides the way. Do not avoid gazing at me, but know me for truly what I am," she says, and you look into her eyes. They seem to be the torches now, bright fires that burn at the heart of the darkness. And you give yourself over to that void. You look into it now, no longer cringing. You let the things you have kept buried, the things you cannot bring yourself to speak, flow into it. And you feel the immensity of Hekate as well, an ancientness and vastness. We call her a goddess, a woman, a hag, a maiden, but now you feel the vast power she contains, and it is overwhelming. She is primordial, a force of nature.

You blink and it is all gone. You no longer stand in the cave but at the old crossroads, two dirt paths going deeper into a wood in either direction. The moon lights a wooden sign post. Below it other travelers have left out offerings to Hekate. You kneel down and leave the only thing you have to offer, the key you still grasp from the underworld.

You hear the goddess's words on the breeze: "There is no more time left. Choose." And you do. Without another thought, with fear no longer coiling around your heart, you choose one of the paths and begin walking down it.

When I first encountered Hekate, what struck me the most was how ancient she is. She is truly ancient; in a way she feels almost more like a force of nature than anything else. She is primordial. Her presence feels towering to me, fluid yet as solid as stone. In my mind's eye, I picture her as one of those towering stone statues that come to life in the original *Clash of the Titans*. Other times she is the void, a darkness that pulls toward it the outcasts and wanderers of whom she is patron, a darkness that pulls toward it all the things you hold on to but need to release. In a devotional ritual to Hekate I attended, several priestesses were channeling different aspects of the goddess at the same time. Participants were asked to come up to hear a message from Hekate, and when I spoke to the priestess, there was an odd double image. I could see the priestess in her trance, and behind her I saw the void of darkness that was Hekate. It was not the cold void of space, but something more akin to the warm abyss of the womb, with the barest suggestion of a human face in the darkness and eyes that burned with a hot fire like her torches. She reminds me that the gods are more than just the human faces we perceive them as wearing. They are something far vaster and unknowable.

Hekate is at her core, and even within her mythology, primordial. She is older than the gods of Olympus, who themselves show deference to her. She is a Titan, a class of deity that in the Greek cosmology first stepped out of the chaos that created the world. Zeus, the king of the Olympian gods, is most well-known for defeating his Titan father, Kronos, and the other Titans in a great war. While he imprisons or destroys the other Titans, he finds no fault in Hekate. In his *Theogony* Hesiod says of her, "She received honour also in starry heaven, and is honoured exceedingly by the deathless gods. For to this day, whenever anyone of men on earth offers rich sacrifices and prays for favour according to custom, he calls upon Hecate.... Also, because she is an only child, the goddess receives not less honour, but much more still, for Zeus honours her." [17]

Hekate is known, among other things, as a goddess of magic, the night, crossroads, witchcraft, and necromancy. She has over twenty titles, *Nyctipolus* (night-wandering), *Atalus* (tender, delicate), *Chthonia* (of the underworld), *Curotrophus* (nurse of the young), *Scylacagetis* (leader of dogs), *Liparocredemnus* (bright-coiffed), *Dadouchos* (torch bearer), and *Propylaia* (before the gate). Although she is often depicted in triple form, her numerous titles and their varied attributes show her to be a deity ruling over a wide range of influence in our lives. Although most modern depictions show her as a crone, most likely due to her connection to the underworld, in many ancient sculptures and depictions Hekate is shown as a maiden or young woman. In Greek vase paintings she is often shown as a woman holding twin torches dressed in a knee-length maiden's skirt and hunting boots, much like Artemis.

It is Hekate who assisted Demeter in her search for Persephone, guiding her through the night with flaming torches. After the mother-daughter reunion, she becomes Persephone's guide as well and her companion while she dwells in Hades. Hekate is associated with borders, crossroads, doorways (especially in city walls), and, in a more liminal sense, the thresholds between the worlds of the dead and the living. It was thought that she could in her more vengeful aspects beset people with evil spirits as well as deter

---

17. Hugh G. Evelyn-White, trans., *The Homeric Hymns and Homerica* (Cambridge: Harvard University Press, 1914), lines 416–30.

harmful spirits from cities or households. Small temples honoring Hekate were placed near the city gates in Byzantium, and when Philip II of Macedon was about to invade the city, it was said that Hekate warned them with the sounds of her sacred dogs and her torches. It had been suggested that Hekate's connection to the dog as one of her sacred animals is in part from the Roman and Greek use of watchdogs for raising alarms, in particular at night.[18] Like the Titaness, "the dog is a creature of the threshold, the guardian of doors and portals, and so it is appropriately associated with the frontier between life and death.... The yawing gates of Hades were guarded by the monstrous watchdog Cerberus, whose function was to prevent the living from entering the underworld and the dead from leaving it."[19] Female dogs were particularly sacred to Hekate. One myth tells of how Queen Hekabe of Troy leapt into the sea after seeing her city fall and Hekate, taking pity on the queen, transformed her into a dog, who served the goddess as her familiar. Other animals associated with her, sometimes with the goddess depicted as having the heads of said animals, include the boar, cow, serpent, and horse.[20]

Sin-Eating

Hekate has the distinction of not just being a goddess but also a Titaness. Several generations of the Greek gods overthrew their predecessors: Uranus was overthrown by his son Kronos, who was in turn overthrown by his son Zeus. Each generation of deities stepped further away from being forces of primordial energy to the more civilized gods, the Olympians. Yet Hekate remains a constant in it all, having the respect of both the gods (of each subsequent generation) and mortals alike. And perhaps it's that closeness to the primordial that is part of this. Hekate stands in the vast chaos, like a black hole that pulls bits of the universe and yourself toward her. I have met more than one devotee to this queen of the underworld who has described her as a sin-eater, and in many ways she is one.

---

18. Hugh McBeath, *The Esoteric Codex: Titans* (Lulu.com, 2016), p. 36.

19. Richard Cavendish, *The Powers of Evil in Western Religion, Magic and Folk Belief* (London: Putnam, 1975), p. 62.

20. Clifton Helmsing, *The Esoteric Codex: Deities of Night* (Lulu.com, 2015), p. 14.

To see Hekate in this context we have to consider the meanings of sin and sin-eating. For many people, part of becoming a Pagan and leaving mainstream monotheism involves a rejection of concepts like sin. Just because there is no concept of sin within Paganism does not mean that we don't have to deal with things like the consequences of our mistakes, our failures, and the self-doubts that weigh on us because of them. We use different vernacular and relate to these concepts in different ways but that doesn't make it any less part of our existence.

The term "sin-eater" is thought to originate in southern England, where the folk custom describes a person who takes on the sins of the dead.[21] English antiquarian and philosopher John Aubrey described the practice in 1686: "The Manner was that when the Corps was brought out of the house and layd on the Biere; a Loafe of bread was brought out, and delivered to the Sinne-eater over the corps, as also a Mazar-bowle of maple (Gossips bowle) full of beer, wch he was to drinke up, and sixpence in money, in consideration whereof he tooke upon him (ipso facto) all the Sinnes of the Defunct, and freed him (or her) from walking after they were dead."[22] There is also the Aztec goddess Tlazoltéotl, who, if one confessed misdeeds to her, was thought to cleanse the soul by eating its filth. The difference here is that while the sin-eater of English folklore performs this function at the end of life, Hekate becomes a cleaning force while we are still in life. She cleanses us of the things that prevent us from moving on within our lives rather than the ones that prevent us from finding peace in death. It is certainly not her only role or function, but it is very much part of her being. There are times when we must release and let go of the things we find at fault with ourselves, release the baggage that comes with our decisions. More often than not, it is more about allowing ourselves to be at peace with ourselves, rather than negotiating penance with a deity. Hekate provides an avenue for us to do that, to look into the void and release the pain of the past or the unhealthy expectations we place upon ourselves.

---

21. Bertram S. Puckle, *Funeral Customs: Their Origin and Development* (London: T. Werner Laurie, 1926; CreateSpace Independent Publishing Platform, 2013), p. 49. Citations refer to the CreateSpace edition.

22. John Aubrey, *Remaines of Gentilisme and Judaisme*, ed. James Britten (London: The Folk-Lore Society, 1881), p. 35.

The closest concept to sin, as we think of it today, in the Greek mind would have been miasma. *Miasma* essentially is a contagious power that can take on a life of its own. It is an impurity that can be caused by an individual's or a community's actions. Until the proper sacrifices are made and the impurity is purged, the wrongdoer, or even an entire society, was thought to be infected and catastrophes would ensue: "There was in Greek belief, no such thing as non-contagious religious danger. Some dangers were more commonly seen as communicable by contact, while others rather threatened the guilty party's descendants.... Every member of any community, therefore, in principle lived under the threat of suffering for his neighbors' offences. The ways in which divine anger against a community could be expressed were diverse."[23] The contamination of miasma was thought to have infected the family of Atreus and was considered the root cause of several violent crimes, one leading to and compounding another.

Hekate exists on the fringes of her own society, being both one of the gods and something more ancient than the Olympians. And she in turn rules over the misfits of mankind, those who live on the fringes. I see her very much in this role as Hekate Nycti-polus (night-wandering), and I see her as ruling over not just the fringes of ourselves but the fringes within us, the parts within us that don't always fit or are messy. Those parts of ourselves often live just on the edge of our perception, a liminal space Hekate knows well. This could also be considered our shadow, containing all the things we are afraid or ashamed of in ourselves. In Greek terms, she can aid us in purifying ourselves from the miasma of our actions and society's.

Hekate stands in the abyss, in the depths of the underworld's darkness. She is the force that takes the barriers away so we may make decisions, so we can choose one path or the other at the crossroads, so we can change, so we are no longer stagnant. She is the force behind it, yet it is up to us to choose, to let her eat our sins and take them into her own darkness. Like Hekate guiding Persephone, she can only show us the way. She can't walk the path for us, but she will be a guide in the dark.

---

23. Robert Parker, *Miasma: Pollution and Purification in Early Greek Religion* (Oxford: Clarendon Press, 1996), p. 257.

Devotional Work and Offerings for Hekate

The Athenians honored Hekate each month with the deipnon. *Deipnon* means "evening meal" or the last meal of the day, and food was placed out for Hekate and the restless dead. This offering was both to purify the household, atoning for any misdeed a member of the household had committed, as well as to engender Hekate's favor and appease the vengeance of any of the spirits that resided with her. Meals were set outside at crossroads or in shrines dedicated to her outside entranceways to the home. The playwright Aristophanes says of these meals, "Ask Hekate whether it is better to be rich or starving; she will tell you that the rich send her a meal every month and that the poor make it disappear before it is even served."[24] Presumably, the poor ate the food left out for the goddess, and given her connection to those who lived on the outskirts of society this makes a kind of sense.

The deipnon was done on the last day of the Athenian calendar, and some modern devotees have adopted it as a monthly practice honoring her. It is important to note that the Attic, or Athenian calendar, was different than calendars of neighboring city-states. The Greek city-states had unique calendars, by which they held religious ceremonies and the daily business of the city-state, making it difficult to match Ancient Greek dates to modern dates. The Attic calendar began in summer after the solstice and followed the moon cycles, while others began after the winter solstice or in the fall. In the Attic calendar the deipnon marked the end of their monthly lunar calendar and fell on the new moon.

Regardless of whether you wish to practice the deipnon on the last day of the month or on the new moon, it is a good way to honor Hekate and purify the home. It is a time when old offerings should be taken off the altar and left outside if possible. I leave a portion of the meal that night on her altar and then place it outside as soon as night falls or the next evening. It is also a good time to clean the altars in the house and clean both your physical space as well as your mental one.

---

24. Aristophanes, *Plutus: The God of Riches,* trans. Henry Fielding (Radford: SMK Books, 2011), line 410.

....
Invocation to Hekate of the Gates

Hekate
One Who Stands at the Gates
Lady of the Crossroads
Night-Wanderer
I invoke thee
Nocturnal one of the saffron robe
Torches in hand, you light the way
A choice to make at the crossroads
The darkness of the underworld to fare
Titaness, keeper of the keys of all the universe
Show me the way
Help me unlock the parts of myself that I have kept hidden
Help me unlock the path before me
That I may walk it
Not in fear, but with you at my side

....
Drawing in Hekate
BY GINA GRASSO

I am older than they say
I am the conception of time
And will be there at the demise of all

I am the governor of all your crossroads
I am the footsteps along your path
And carry you when you can no longer walk

I am the brightest star in the night sky
I am the universe within
And the darkness without

I am magick in all things

I am poison of no things

And cure to life and transform death

Know me now by this name, Hekate

....

Ritual for Insight in Choosing a Path

You Will Need:

Black candle

Old key

Two of Swords from a tarot deck of your choice

Offering to Hekate

Use this ritual when you need to make a choice and wish to ask for Hekate's help in making sense of the situation and for a positive outcome. If you choose, you can cast a circle in whatever manner or tradition you like.

Light the candle, invoke Hekate, and see her standing before you. Place the key and the Two of Swords on the altar and ask Hekate to help you choose a path. Ask her to help you make a choice and for a good outcome. Ask for clarity in making your choice. Say,

Hekate

Lady of the Crossroads

Help me make a choice

To choose the right path

To see clearly the consequences of my choices

I stand at the crossroads

Stand beside me, mighty Hekate

Let me not stand still but take action

Take a moment to connect to Hekate. Ask for advice or how to handle the situation. When you are ready, thank her and leave the offering. Let the candle burn out, or if it is a larger candle, let it burn out over the course of the next few days in a fire-safe container.

....
Hekate Black Salt

There are many different recipes for black salt. This is a variation you can use for protection or getting rid of a problem or person while calling upon Hekate's energies. Black salt is traditionally used in Hoodoo to protect a home by sprinkling it around the property to keep the home safe from troublemakers. It is also used to drive away evil spirits or the mortal kind by sprinkling it in the footprints of a bothersome person. For our purposes it can be sprinkled in front of the door, invoking Hekate's protection as a guardian of the gates. It can also be added to other mixtures for banishment and protection when calling on Hekate.

There are two ways you can make your black salt. Traditionally, scrapings from a cast-iron skillet make the salt black. Given that iron is thought to ward off things like faeries and in some mythologies is thought to break magic in general, I like the idea of using it for protection. The charred pieces that come off a well-seasoned cast-iron skillet are not going to be all iron but are iron enough to work well. Alternatively, ash from a fire is used and mixed with the salt. The method I prefer is to burn part of the herbs listed in the ingredients list (leaving a handful to mix with the final product) and using the ash to blacken the salt. If you prefer to use the cast-iron scrapings method, simply add a handful of the herbs to mix with your final product.

The herbs I have chosen are some of the many herbs connected to Hekate in the *Argonautica Orphica,* a Greek poem that dates to the fifth or sixth centuries CE that lists a number of herbs that grew in the Garden of Hekate. But you can easily substitute any of the other herbs listed in the poem that call to you, or ones you personally connect with her.

You Will Need:
1 handful juniper berries
3 bay leaves
1 teaspoon ground pepper
Fire-safe bowl
Small bowl of salt
7 drops cypress essential oil

To make the salt, mix the herbs together and put ¾ into a fire-safe bowl. Use a lighter or match to burn the herbs until they are ash. In the bowl add your salt and mix together until the salt turns a dark color. You may need to add more burned herbs until the salt turns the desired color. Add the cypress oil and the rest of the herbs and mix together. As you mix the salt together, see Hekate standing before you, infusing the mixture with her energy and protection. When you are done, store the salt in a jar or plastic bag.

·················

Spell to Hekate to Guard the Boundaries

You Will Need:
Hekate black salt (see page 93)
Old key
Offering to Hekate

This spell can be used to protect literal boundaries, like around a home, or figurative ones, when someone is intruding on your personal boundaries.

If protecting a physical space, sprinkle some of the Hekate black salt in front of the doorway to your home. Alternatively, sprinkle some around the perimeter of the property if you feel the need to do so. Near the doorway dig a small hole, large enough for the key to fit in. Sprinkle more of the salt in the hole. Then, holding the key in your hands, see in your mind a larger-than-life Hekate towering over the home, blocking entrance to all who wish you harm. Her flaming torches burn those who get near and are not welcome. Two black dogs at either of her sides howl and then bound off to walk the boundaries of your property, protecting it. Say,

> *Hekate*
> *Propylaia, One Before the Gates*
> *Guard the boundaries*
> *Key bearer*
> *Stand between myself and harm*
> *May your hounds cry out in warning*
> *May your flames shine bright*
> *May I be circled in your protection*
> *A circle unending*

Unbending
Hekate
One before the gates
Let none pass who wishes me harm
Protect the boundaries, mighty Hekate!

Place the key in the ground and bury it. To renew your protections every so often, put more salt around the front door and see Hekate standing guard there. Leave Hekate an offering thanking her for her protection.

If you are protecting your personal boundaries, place the salt and the key in a small bag and carry it on your person when you feel like you need protection or when dealing with a person who pushes your boundaries.

....

Ritual to Purify Miasma

Miasma is a difficult concept to wrap our minds around. It is similar to sin, but not at all the same concept. It can be an impurity of a person through their actions or something that infects and has sway over a community from the actions of many. In the Greek context it can even be the deeds of one's ancestors that causes the miasma and not one's own sins as it were. In this context we will look at it as "pollution." Whether you feel guilt over something, feel shame, have been around people who make you feel "polluted," or feel like the negativity of others around you is starting to rub off on yourself, these are all good times to purify.

Greek ritual practice often involved washing, particularly to wash off the impurity and dirt of the day's labors. We will use a similar concept here to purify. It does not need to be done as a full ritual, but it can be something you use in daily or monthly practices in conjunction with honoring Hekate.

You Will Need:
Large bowl
Water
Rosemary sprigs
Wine or another offering to Hekate

Create sacred space in your usual manner. Call quarters or cast a circle if you wish. Invoke Hekate in whatever manner feels correct to you. Place the bowl on the altar. Pour the water into the bowl and lay the sprigs of rosemary in the water. Say,

Hekate, sin-eater

Hekate, Night-Wanderer

Older than the gods themselves

I call to you for purification

I wash my hands clean before you

I wash my soul of all that pollutes it

I wash away the troubles of the day

Hekate, cleanse me

That no pollution may touch me

That the pollution of others may not be upon me

Cleanse and protect me, mighty Hekate!

See a bright light filling the water; see it as the purest, most sparkling water possible. Use the sprigs to sprinkle the water on your body. If working with a group, have one person move around the circle using the rosemary to sprinkle the water on participants. Afterward, wash your hands in the water, seeing all that "pollutes" you washing away with the water and flowing away.

Thank Hekate and leave her the offering you have brought. I prefer to use wine, but you can leave whatever offering feels correct to you. After the ritual, pour the water outside or down the drain; do not use it for anything else.

8

Sedna

It is cold and you wrap the oiled seal hide around your shoulders closer to keep out the wind. The sounds of the ocean surround you as you and your companions drift on the waves in a boat. It has been a long time since you saw the shore or anyone had a sense of which direction leads to safety. Some of the others are huddled on the other side of the boat, discussing what should be done. Some think an offering must be made so the gods will bring the ship home. You are too cold and tired to have an opinion. You huddle in your skin until the others come over to you. One, a friend of yours, greets you and begins asking you something, while the others circle behind you. You begin to answer when you suddenly realize what is happening. With a great rush, they shove you over the edge and into the water.

The water is icy and the current strong. It rips you away from the boat before you can try to scramble back aboard. And you realize your friends have abandoned you: you are their offering so they may get home safely. With this realization you feel heavy and don't even fight the current. Still gripping your sealskin, you let yourself sink. Down and down you go, deeper and deeper. You grasp the sealskin and sink and sink. Soon you start to see fish and seals swim by. They look at you, curious. Deeper and deeper you go. Something tells you to wrap yourself in the skin, to bring it about your shoulder, and you listen to the instinct. As you do so, you feel yourself changing. The skin and your own flesh begin to merge. Your shape shifts, and your hands become flippers. And you find yourself transformed into a seal. You swim easily now and see other seals coming close to swim alongside you.

Two seals swim by you and then dive deeper into the darkness toward the sea floor. You sense they want you to follow them, and you do. The water is murky and dark. Soon you can only see *a few feet ahead of you. The seals lead you to the entrance of a small cave, look back at you, and then dart inside.*

After a few minutes the pitch black of the cave gives way to a gray light. You emerge from the cave a human again, with the sealskin wrapped around your shoulders. The other side of the cave leads to a gray landscape. You know you are below the ocean floor, yet this place is a long stretch of gray sky and bare grasslands. There are patches of snow here and there, and there is a small hut in the distance, with a fire burning inside. You are still cold and the promise of warmth makes you start walking toward the hut.

There is a mist that surrounds the grasslands, and you think you see other figures in the mist. But they remain in the mist and do not bother you. The sun seems to shine in the sky above, but it is covered by gray clouds.

Soon you come to the entrance of the hut, and you can feel the warmth of the fire even from outside. You call out, asking to come in. A voice welcomes you, and you bend your head and step into the hut. The firelight dances all around the small wooden structure, giving it a warm glow. A woman sits by the fire, tending it. She looks up and smiles at you. Her eyes are dark, and you feel like you can see the dark swells of the sea in them. Her hair is jet black and knotted in places, with seaweed and other debris in it.

She welcomes you to sit by the fire and you do. It is then that you notice that her hands are bound in heavy cloth. Here and there stains of blood have seeped through the bandages. You ask then if you can help her. She has given you warmth and welcome, and you wish to return the kindness. She smiles and lets you take a stick she was tending the fire with from her. You add more wood to the fire, and soon it is roaring and pleasantly hot in the hut. You turn then to the woman and ask if you can comb her hair. Smiling again she lets you use a bone comb to take the tangles out of her long dark hair. You take seaweed and other ocean debris from the strands. As you do, she tells you of all the animals who live in the ocean, those that come to visit her, and the ones she watches over. She sounds so loving, so concerned with those that live in this realm. You begin to wonder how she hurt her hands. Who would harm this woman? And then you realize this is Sedna, the goddess who created the animals of the oceans from her severed fingers. Sedna, who was betrayed by those she loved most.

She seems to notice your gaze resting on her hands. "Even the gods know betrayal. When those we trusted turn their backs on us, when we put our trust in the wrong people, these betrayals become wounds to our spirits. They make us seek solitude and forget that at times we need others.

No matter how much we resist it, we need each other," she says. You are reminded of your friends who pushed you off the boat and other times you felt the sting of betrayal.

"Do not close yourself off from the world," she tells you. "Trust your judgment and learn from your failings, but do not let them drown you." She looks at her hands. "Our fears can cripple us, prevent us from healing if we do not learn from them." The bandages fall off, revealing worn but healed hands. She runs them through her straightened hair. "If we close ourselves off, we will never find those worthy of our trust. Leave your wounded self here and allow yourself to return to the world made whole."

She gestures for you to throw the sealskin into the fire, and after a moment's hesitation, you do so. At first the burning skin sends up the smell of salt and ocean into the air, reminding you of the ship and those who tossed you overboard. But the smell fades and you watch the fire for some time, knowing you are letting the wounds of the past burn away. The skin kept you warm but it separated you from others. You hide yourself away, protecting yourself from getting close to others. It kept you warm and secure, but it isolated you as well. The wall you have built between you and others burns away with it. And you know you no longer have to hide within yourself.

Sedna puts her hands on your shoulders, and you begin to feel light. The hut fades away until you are surrounded by white light and have returned to the world above, whole and safe.

Sedna is the Inuit goddess who rules over the sea, sea mammals, and the monsters of the depths. She was known by a number of names and titles across Alaska, Canada, and Greenland, including *Nuliajuk, Immap Ukuua* (Mother of the Sea), *Takanakapsaluk* (The Terrible One Down Under), and *Unigumisuitok* (The One Who Does Not Want a Husband).[25] She was thought to be the mother of the sea and its animals, hiding fish and game from hunters when they did not appease her or show proper respect to the game they hunted. She was also credited with being able to control storms.

There are several versions of how Sedna came to rule over the ocean and its animals. In one version Sedna is a beautiful young woman who rejects all of her many suitors. This angers her father, and when a hunter from another village comes to visit, he gives

---

25. Patricia Ann Lynch, *Native American Mythology A to Z,* 2nd ed., Mythology A to Z (New York: Chelsea House, 2010), p. 99.

the girl a sleeping potion and gives her to the hunter in exchange for some fish. But the hunter is actually a great bird (the type of bird varies with the story, sometimes a sea bird, a raven, or a fulmar) disguised in the shape of a man, and he takes Sedna to a large nest on top of a cliff. Her father comes to rescue her, but when the great bird returns and sees his bride has been stolen, he asks a sea spirit to call up a great storm to stop the father and daughter from reaching the shore. In desperation Sedna's father throws her over the side of kayak, hoping to appease the sea's rage. When Sedna attempts to cling on to the kayak, her father takes his axes and chops her fingers off. Each digit transforms into the different species of animals who live in the ocean. The final blow he delivers to her head sends her sinking to the sea bottom. In one version her fingers freeze and fall off. In another version Sedna is so dissatisfied with the suitors her father presents that she marries a dog. Enraged, her father takes her out to sea and throws her overboard, chopping off her fingers as she clings to the side of the kayak.

In yet another telling of Sedna's story humans have no game to hunt and exist only by eating the earth. It is not a good life, and when the bird suitor comes to the village, he tells her he will bring her to his village where the tents have no holes and there is good food to eat. She agrees to leave with him, but when they arrive, she finds he has tricked her, his village is worse than her own, and her bird husband treats her poorly. When her father comes to visit, he sees her unhappiness and takes her in his kayak. When Sedna's bird husband discovers her missing, he uses his wings to stir up the waves of a storm. Again, fearing for himself, her father throws her overboard, chopping off her fingers, which transform into not just the animals of the sea but all the animals of the earth. This gives the people something to eat other than clods of earth, yet there is a price. The animals are of Sedna's flesh and thus of their own flesh, and certain taboos must be upheld. If the taboos of the hunt are not respected, then the animal's spirit will return to Sedna and tell her of the people's disrespect, and she will withhold game animals from the hunters. In this version Sedna, surviving the storm, returns to her village and to her father's hut. She chops off his feet and hands in her anger, and the earth opens up, bringing them to the underworld.[26]

---

26. Franz Boas. *The Central Eskimo* (Lincoln: University of Nebraska Press, 1972), p. 60.

In the Netsilik region Sedna is called Nuliajuk and is an orphan who is teased by the other children. When the tribe leaves for another hunting ground, the other children push her from their kayak into the sea, chopping off her fingers as she tries to pull herself out of the water. Regardless of the variations of Sedna's transformation into a goddess, the themes of being thrown overboard and mutilated by someone she should be able to trust remain.

Although Sedna sinks to the ocean floor, she does not die. She becomes transformed into a goddess, and her missing fingers become seals and other ocean life. As a goddess, Sedna's realm was both the ocean and its inhabitants as well as Adlivun, the Inuit underworld. In Inuit mythology Adlivun (meaning "those who live beneath us") refers to both the Inuit underworld itself and the spirits who live there. It is usually described as a frozen wasteland located beneath both the land and the sea, and spirits must dwell there for a year to be purified before they can travel to the Quidlivun (Land of the Moon), where they can find their final peace.

In addition to not showing the proper respect when hunting, other transgressions of humankind also affected Sedna. Immoral behavior and acts enraged her and were thought to "make her beautiful black hair wild and disheveled. Taboo violations [would] plug her eyes and ears with debris." [27] In her anger she withheld the sea's animals from hunters and let the people starve. The only way to appease her was for a shaman, or *angakoq* (the Iglulik called shamans *nakazoq* or "one who drops down to the bottom of the sea"), to go to the spirit world, where Sedna dwelled, and comb Sedna's hair and clean her face since she had no fingers to do so herself. The shaman would then question the goddess about what transgressions had caused her state. After braiding her hair, the shaman's spirit would return to the mortal world, a "public confirmation of ... transgressions" would occur, and in exchange Sedna would let the animals of the ocean return. [28]

---

27. Kimberly C. Patton, *The Sea Can Wash Away All Evils: Modern Marine Pollution and the Ancient Cathartic Ocean* (New York: Columbia University Press, 2007), p 80.

28. Ibid.

Learning from Betrayal and Judgment

The thing about betrayal is it isn't the actual event that breaks you. We all have experienced betrayal of some kind, whether it is by friends, loved ones, or family. The majority of the time we can recover from the actual circumstance of the betrayal, but betrayal keeps hurting long after the actual event because it keeps replaying in our heads, and it destroys our ability to trust or put our faith in others. We are left asking, "Why?" Why were we betrayed in the first place? And we begin to withdraw our trust of others who haven't harmed us simply because we see with new eyes that they have the potential to betray us as well. We recede like Sedna to the dark bottom of the ocean, we recoil into ourselves and vow never to let anyone close again.

In many ways people put their faith in Sedna. In the harsh climate occupied by the Inuit, with millions of square miles of tundra and icy coasts, agriculture is nearly impossible and hunting and trapping are the primary source of food. A good hunt is important and can mean life or death. Making offerings for a good hunt to Sedna and relying on her that they might find game and not starve when, we can assume, she by every right can no longer put her faith in others after experiencing so much betrayal shows a kind of symmetry. She is betrayed more than once. She is first betrayed when her father gives her a sleeping draft and gives her to the stranger, angered by her defiance of his wish for her to marry. Then she is betrayed yet again after trusting him to rescue her and he chooses to toss her overboard to save himself from the sea spirit's rage. Even deeper is the betrayal when he chops off her fingers as she tries to lift herself back into the boat. She chooses to trust him again, only to learn the hard way that her trust is misplaced. The consequences of those betrayals leave her wounded. Yet instead of drowning she is transformed, creating life out of her mangled fingers, and she herself becomes powerful, guiding souls through Adlivun and to final peace. Sedna's lesson is not so much making peace with betrayal but learning discernment and judgment.

As much as we don't like to admit it, we have to trust people. We trust our mechanic to fix our car, our banks not to steal our money. We have to trust when we drive down the road that the other cars will drive in the right lanes. We have to trust people to function, yet we can't give our trust away blindly. We have to judge people. This sounds simple but has deep consequences. When we enter the underworld, there is always an element of judgment. Our guides evaluate if we are ready to move on to other challenges. A function of most underworld gods involves judgment. Anubis weighs and judges the hearts of the dead on the scales, and not everyone gets into the Norse Valhalla, only the brave.

Sedna teaches us that learning to trust again requires judgment. That we must heal, or we risk closing ourselves off to the world forever. Judgment and discernment can only come from being betrayed, in learning to heal yourself from the injuries caused to you. You don't have to forgive the person who has wronged you, but you do have to be willing to learn whom to open up to and whom not to. Despite being betrayed, Sedna became more powerful for it. She learns discernment and guides others through their sorrow in the underworld of Adlivum before they can go to final peace in the Land of the Moon. And she asks those who ask for her blessing, whether it is for the hunt or otherwise, to trust her as well.

Devotional Work and Offerings for Sedna

I offer Sedna parts of every meal when I work with her. It can be small parts, not the entire plate. In the morning I will discard the food. I thank Sedna for giving the people food through her own flesh, thanking her for her sacrifice. I have the habit of finding bones and making art or jewelry out of them and will often ask her to help me to make sure the animal's spirit is at peace and know how to best honor them in whatever I create. It was thought that the spirit of the hunted animal resided in the village for three days, ensuring that the gifts of the meat and fur were given the proper respect, and if they were not, the animal's spirit would return to Sedna and report the misdeeds of the hunters. In a similar respect I ask her how best to honor the remains of the animal bones I work with.

Sedna is also a good ally for learning to trust others and oneself again and for seeking forgiveness for our own transgressions. Other than offering food from meals, I prefer to leave offerings to her in the ocean if possible or in moving water.

....
Invocation to Sedna

Sedna
Mother of the Deep

Lady of the Oceans
Terrible One
You who rule over those who live beneath us
Sedna, who knew betrayal
Teach me to judge wisely
To know whom to give my trust to
And whom to withdraw it from

....

A Release of Transgressions

Sedna can be called upon for both releasing transgressions and being able to allow ourselves to trust again and for justice for misdeeds. The next spell will explore this further. For this one, you travel to Sedna's realm to wash away the betrayals that stay with you.

You Will Need:

Water

Salt

Small dish

Offering to Sedna

You may wish to do this near the ocean or a body of water. Mix the water and salt together in the dish. Put a little of the mixture on your tongue, taste the salt, and think of Sedna's realm—the feel of the ocean, the push of the waves, the way the water tastes. Then anoint your brow, hands, and feet with the water. Give your offering to Sedna, saying these or similar words:

Sea Woman
You who survived treachery
Your severed fingers creating new life from betrayal
I feel your grief
I leave you this offering in gratitude

Find a comfortable place to sit or lie down. If you like, you might wish to play drumming music in the background. For journey work I tend to prefer something with a heartbeat rhythm to it. Say,

Sedna, I go to your realm,
I drop down to the bottom of the sea
I enter your realm of ice and cold
I travel to you in Adlivun

See yourself traveling to the ocean. You step into the waters, not swimming but walking beneath the depths, the sand beneath your feet. Soon the water covers your head but you can still breathe without problems. You walk and walk, deeper and deeper, until you are somewhere past the depths of the ocean, in a land of ice and darkness. There is a hut there with an oil lamp light and you go to it. You speak with Sedna. You tell her of your grief and ask her how you may release these things and move past them. Spend as long as you like speaking and connecting with Sedna.

....

Justice for Transgressions

There are times when justice is needed for the wrongs done against us. It doesn't mean we should withdraw within ourselves and forget how to trust again, but asking for justice for ourselves can also be appropriate.

You Will Need:

Paper

Pen

Jar

Seawater (or water mixed with salt)

Nori (or leaves and twigs)

On the paper write the situation or name of the person. Spend a few minutes seeing the piece of paper and the person merging, becoming the same. Put the piece of paper in the jar and fill it with the seawater. Mixing tap water with table salt is perfectly fine too. You can use dried leaves and twigs or any other debris found in the yard or around the house to represent the impurity you are asking Sedna to bring justice for, as Sedna's hair was thought to be dirtied by such things when people behaved unjustly. If you can't find nori or seaweed (found in most health-food stores), you can also use leaves, as they look reminiscent of hair when floating in water, and are from Sedna's realm.

Hold the jar and see Sedna standing before you upon a raging ocean, the wind blowing, the waves dark and crashing. Say,

Sea Woman

Mother who observes the taboos of the people

Your hair is dirty, the actions of _____ fill you with rage

Your eyes and ears fill with the treachery of _____

I ask for justice

I ask you who were once wronged

Bring justice, Mother of the Sea

Bring justice

May there be no sustenance for _____

No succor

No safe harbor

No place to turn to where your rage does not touch them

Sedna, sea woman

Mother who observed the taboos of the people

Let it be so

Bury the jar, near a body of water if possible.

Part 3
Challenge

The brick walls are there for a reason.
The brick walls are not there to keep us out.
The brick walls are there to give us a chance to show how badly we want something.
—Randy Pausch, *The Last Lecture*

Taking the first steps into the dark of the underworld can be terrifying, but it's the easy part. Now the battle truly begins. Once we have accepted that we must change, or that it's inevitable, we begin to traverse the underworld itself, facing the demons and shadows that live there. But like Campbell's reluctant hero, there are allies in the dark too, guides to show us the way as we confront what lies in the underworld's depths. The goddesses in this section are ones connected to breaking down barriers and taking action toward change.

The phase of challenge is all about doing. In the descent we mourn and look at the reasons why we need to change and shed our illusions, while the challenge phase is all about enacting that change. Choosing to embrace change can be terrifying. It is the Fool jumping off the cliff into the unknown. There are no more chances to go back. The only choice left is whether or not you want to grow and become stronger. The alternative is to lie down and stay stagnant. Are you willing to suffer the pain that allows you to transform?

Buddhist teacher, author, and nun Pema Chödrön recounts advice she received from one of her Buddhist mentors when she felt she had hit rock bottom that perfectly describes the struggle of the challenge. He told her what she was going though was like walking into the ocean and being knocked down by a wave. She had the choice to lie there and drown or get up again and continue walking. He didn't promise that there would be no more waves or that she wouldn't end up flat on her back again, but that eventually the waves would seem to get smaller and smaller. Chödrön explains, "You begin to have the ability to hold what I call 'the rawness of vulnerability' in your heart.... When these [waves] happen in your life, they become a source of growth, a source of forward.... The waves that are knocking you down begin to appear smaller and have less and less of an ability to knock you over. And actually maybe it is the same wave, maybe it's even a bigger wave than the one that hit last year, but it appears to you smaller because of your ability to swim with it or ride the wave." [29] It isn't that we stop struggling or facing challenges; it's how we go about facing the challenge that matters. Crisis brings out our true nature; it's a catalyst for change. As we work with the goddesses in this section, take time to think about how you face crises. How do you approach the challenges you face?

Sometimes we are halfway through the process and just get stuck. We don't stand up to the challenge that lies before us and wish the gods could just make our lives better without all the hassle we are going through. But when our reluctant hero is in the underworld, in many ways they are being judged. Will they face the task before them? Or will they run? Their underworldly guides are always there in the shadows, ready to intervene if needed, but at the same time letting the hero fight their own battles, conquer their own demons. They are worthy of aid only when they take action and face the challenge.

All too often we treat the gods as spiritual vending machines. A little incense or some wine poured in a bowl becomes the cosmic quarter that drops down whatever we want from the sky. The gods can do amazing things, but we have to earn them too. We have to still make the mundane efforts to get what we want. They won't do all the work for you, and neither will they ask something of you that you can't accomplish. When you enter the underworld, the gods judge you too. Not everyone gets to go to Valhalla, and sometimes people get lost in the underworld.

The gods challenge us all the time. Seeing them as divine parents who always help us out when we need it is part of our problem with accepting this. We don't like to think of the gods as causing us any harm in any way. Placing a challenge in front of us isn't harmful per se, but it isn't hand-holding either. When we ask for something, the gods may challenge our worthiness. In many ways they are seeing if we can prove that we are worthy of something by fulfilling the challenge. I don't think the gods put a challenge

---

29. Pema Chödrön, "How to Move Forward Once You've Hit Bottom," *Lion's Roar: Buddhist Wisdom for Our Time* (blog), October 21, 2016, http://www.lionsroar.com/how-to-move-forward-once-youve-hit-bottom/.

in front of us that we aren't capable of accomplishing, but they make us work for it all the same.

When we start our journey, it is very easy to get caught up in the process, to delve so deeply in feelings that may have been repressed for a long time that we forget that the purpose we started out with was to move past them. We forget that we journey through our own underworlds in order to come back to the world of light again. It is easy to get caught in self-examination. We know we need to change—we talk about it and maybe even have others supporting or sympathizing with us—but we are afraid to actually move on to taking action. The problem with taking that final step off the cliff to transformation, that moment when you enact change instead of just thinking about it, is that there are no guarantees. We don't know if we are going to fail or succeed. We don't know if our choice will make us any happier or unhappier than we are now. The unknown is horribly scary. We hate it. But it is just one of the challenges we must face. The alternative is to remain stuck.

The goddesses in this section are all about taking action, whether it be facing our fears or making changes. They will challenge you. They will judge you and evaluate if you are ready to move on. And in many cases you may work with them for quite a while before you feel that you have worked through their lessons.

9

OYA

It is dusk and you find yourself on a winding path that leads to a graveyard. Take a moment to look at how the graveyard appears. What do the gates look like? Is there a stone wall that surrounds the grounds that belong to the dead? What do the trees look like that grow around its border? Is it an ancient graveyard or a modern one?

You walk up to the graveyard's gate and stand silently for a moment asking the spirits who guard this place if you may enter, for you are seeking the goddess Oya, and this is one of her sacred places. After a few minutes you feel a sense of welcoming, and after placing nine shiny pennies on the ground by the gate, you push the gate open and step inside. You walk among the gravestones, reading the names and messages on those that catch your eye. Some may be familiar to you, and if you feel moved to do so, spend a few moments speaking to and honoring the spirits who rest there.

It begins to grow darker, and you notice there are candles lit near some of the stones, some even burning on top of them. And in the dim light of the fading day, you begin to see ghostly figures among the stones. It is the shades and spirits who dwell here. They all seem to be moving toward the center of the graveyard, their focus captured by something, pulling them like a magnet.

In the sky you see the flash of lightning, a long strike that paints a jagged line of light from high in the sky to the ground. Thunder rumbles in the distance. And you too feel the urge to walk toward the center of the graveyard. With the spirits you walk among the stones until you come to the base of a small hill. There are no stones on it, but someone has left out baskets of food and other offerings, along with many candles that burn like fireflies in the fading light.

On the hill is a woman. She is tall and lean and muscular. Her skin is ebony, and she wears a skirt with many bright colors that shift and catch the air as she dances fiercely. There is no music, but she dances to a rhythm that's deep in her own soul. You cannot hear the tune, but you can feel it in the way she moves and in the sound of the wind and thunder. The wind has picked up too, and it blows her skirts. The air feels charged with the smell and energy of a storm, and dark clouds gather overhead. The air tastes like rain, even though the drops have not started. There is a kind of storm in her dance. Her hands move as if they wield weapons: they fight a fierce battle one moment, then they change to a joyful celebration the next, and then her mad twirling is the eye of a storm and the winds of a hurricane. There is fierceness and joy, intermingled in every move and gesture she makes, and it is entrancing and invigorating at the same time.

To see her better, you move closer till you stand not far away from the woman alone at the crest of the hill. She stands tall suddenly, a hand outstretched to the sky. As she does so, a bolt of lightning flashes down from the sky, and to your astonishment she catches it, wielding and swinging it around like a spear in her hand. She laughs madly with joy, and then she looks straight at you and beckons you with her free hand. "Well what are you waiting for? Come! Dance!"

And you do. You dance to the sounds of the storm, to the electricity in the air, to the beat of your own hammering heart, to the drumbeat of the wind that sounds like a war cry. At first it is slow, and then like Oya you dance faster and faster, your movements becoming wild like the storm churning overhead, until finally you can dance no more and collapse on the ground. You feel like a child who has twirled around in circles too long and made themselves feel dizzy, yet there is still a joyful smile on your face. Oya laughs again, and, tossing the lightning back into the sky, she comes over to peer down at you, hands on her hips, a smile on her face.

"You danced well. Not everyone is brave enough to do so. Not everyone can understand that battle is a dance, sometimes a joyful one and other times an angry one, and the storm is our own will that drives it. When you become the storm, unfettered and free, your will a singular force as sharp and bright as lightning, then nothing can stand in your way. Then you will know you are invincible and free, and because you believe it, it will be so." You watch as she calms the winds with a gesture, and the storm calms and the skies clear. The spirits calm as well and begin to drift away into the graveyard. "I am the guardian of the graveyard gates, and I am the storm and the winds. I go to war when I please. And I guard the graveyard and dwell in the marketplace, changing fortunes like the wind. I am change; will you welcome me or fear me? Will you greet me with joy or terror? What do you choose?"

You think of places in your own life you need to welcome change and the reasons you fear or resist it. You think of the ghosts of the past you hold on to without letting them be shed from your being. You think of one area you can welcome change into gladly. And you walk over to the offer-

ings and leave one of your own. See it clearly in your hands. Place it in one of the baskets, and then ask Oya to help you in this change and to welcome it with joyfulness.

Oya is the fierce and powerful warrior orisha who rules over storms, the marketplace, and the gates of the cemetery in Santería and Yoruba traditions. In Yoruba *Oya* means "she tore." Her epithets include Mother of Nine, as the Niger, her sacred river, has nine tributaries. She is also *Ayaba Nikua* (Queen of Death) and *Ayi Lo Da* (She Who Turns and Changes). Oya is a force of swift change, wielding lightning and controlling the winds of storms. Machete in one hand and fly whip in the other, she is a warrior, yet she can also be quite protective and compassionate. She is the orisha to call on when fighting a war of any kind, yet she is also one to go to for renewal.

In Santería the supreme deity and creator of the universe is Olorun. Just below this supreme being are slightly lesser spirits, orisha, who rule over different aspects of life. The orisha require food, sacrifice, and human praise in order to grant petitions and remain powerful. In this sense Oya is not exactly a goddess in the sense of other traditions, though she possesses the powers and abilities of one. Being heavily influenced by Catholicism, Santería and related traditions also equate many of the orisha to particular saints. When it comes down to it, Oya feels no less divine to me than any other deity. The Yoruba hierarchy of divinity is just another way to see or arrange the world of the gods. Whether you call her an orisha or goddess makes little difference as long as you approach her with respect.

Oya is thought to live in the marketplace, changing the fortunes of those gathered there. She also rules over the graveyard, particularly the entrances to graveyards. She will escort sprits to the cemetery gates. Once Oya ruled over the oceans, but she found the temperature of the waters not to her liking and tricked Yemayá into ruling over the oceans and taking the graveyards for herself. At first this angered Yemayá, but she soon learned to love the oceans she still rules over.

Oya's husband is Chango (alternatively, Shango) and there are various versions of their interactions found in Cuba and Africa. In some Chango seduces Oya away from her first husband, Ogun. Chango himself has two previous wives, Oya being his favorite. It is thought Chango cannot go into battle without Oya at his side and that his wife is fiercer in battle than he is.

I see Oya in the dark mass of storm clouds, in the charged way the winds and air feel during a storm, powerful and energized. She is in the taste of the air after a spring storm, and she is the movement, change, and the clearing away of things that only the power behind a storm can be. I've always loved storms. Growing up, I would love nothing better than to listen to a storm as it rolled through our porch, and it was because of a storm that I first met Oya. My plane had been delayed because of a blizzard, and if the storm didn't clear up, it was unlikely my flight was leaving at all. I was a little desperate to get to my destination, running through the possibilities of whom to make offerings to in my head. Something in the howling winds made me call to Oya, and I made my offerings and asked her to redirect or quell the winds she held sway over. I did not expect such a clear response. I could see her clearly before me, confident with a joyful smile on her face. She bargained with me. If I delivered a message for her to someone, she would do as I asked. I agreed, and the next morning I was able to catch another flight without any more obstacles. I delivered the message to a friend whom Oya apparently had her eye on, and from there I began my relationship with Oya, who remains one of the deities I always have an altar for in my home.

Joyful Change and Honoring the Dead

More than any other deity connected to change and transition, Oya teaches us to greet them with joy in our hearts. What struck me the most about Oya in my first encounter with her was the joyfulness that filled her. She wasn't any less fierce or powerful. But she wore her great power, her willingness to go into battle, with a fierce joy. Oya is connected to the wind, and as such she excels at blowing away the old and making room for the new. She can be a gentle breeze or a tornado. She knows change is inevitable and takes pleasure in the process.

When we have moved past the grief that brings us to the doorway of change and accept the process, Oya teaches us to clear away the old with joy in our hearts. She also excels at anything to do with business, as she rules over the marketplace. In this guise she is all business and guile. She is also a good deity to call upon when fighting legal battles or any of life's battles in general.

As a guardian of the graveyard, Oya can also help us honor those who have undergone the more final process of change, death. Honoring the ancestors, both those of blood and those inherited through traditions, was a vital practice in many cultures. Ancestor worship can vary from honoring those we knew in life who have passed to honoring our more distant ancestors whom we have a connection with through blood. We can also connect and work with our ancestors of spirit, those who have become ancestors through a connection within a tradition or culture. For example, some devotees of Celtic deities have adopted Boudicca as an ancestral spirit, even though they have no actual blood connection to the ancient queen. In the same fashion some Pagans in general honor teachers of the Craft who have passed as ancestors of the community.

Working with ancestors can be rewarding and give us a connection to our past. It is also useful for clearing away negative connections that come to us from our ancestors as well. Our ancestors were not necessarily any more enlightened than us while incarnated, and working with them can help us heal issues we have about our own pasts.

The first step to creating a relationship with our ancestors is to create a space for them in our home. Your ancestral altar can be as small or ornate as you like. It can include family pictures of those who have passed, a bowl or other vessel for offerings, and even items that remind you of one who has passed or that the person gave to you in life. If invoking cultural ancestors, you can include items that remind you of that culture. You can ask Oya to guard your altar, as she guards the graveyard entrances, and keep unwanted spirits away.

Leaving offerings and burning candles for the ancestors is not the only way to honor or work with them. We can also ask them to help us in certain tasks or to keep an eye on the home. Ancestors can also bring messages when you start listening to them. On my mother's side of the family my great-grandmother often appears in dreams to different family members, is seen in the house, and in one instance walked up to the front door and rang the bell. Her appearance is usually when "shit is about to hit the fan" as a kind of warning, while her husband appears usually when things are bad but about to get better. During a few Samhain rituals when some family members were not talking to each other, my great-grandmother decided to intervene. She has the habit of appearing and wanting to have messages passed on to family members. She was a very insistent woman in life, thought John Wayne was the definition of what a "real man" should be, and would light a new cigarette and smoke it before she was finished with the last one. She is no different having passed. Once the ancestors know we are listening, they have no problem speaking their mind or showing up when we least expect it.

Devotional Work and Offerings for Oya

Oya enjoys dark-colored things. Offerings to her can include dark pudding, black coffee with sugar, dark rum, chocolate, or things that are black, brown, purple, or burgundy. Eggplant is also a traditional offering to her. Nine is a sacred number to her, and things offered in that number are also good. I often leave nine pennies on her altar, and they make an easy on-the-go offering to her during travel when there is nothing else on hand. When visiting a graveyard, it is good to leave nine pennies or an offering of some kind to Oya at the entrance. When petitioning Oya for something, you can find nine small eggplants (small young ones can be found in most supermarkets). Place them on a plate or in an offering bowl on her altar with nine pennies. I will often carve a symbol into one of the eggplants symbolizing what I am asking her for. Then after a few days (nine if possible), take the eggplant and pennies and leave them near a marketplace, like a farmers' market or a flea market. You can even dispose of the offerings in a garbage can in the market. Some people do not like to throw out offerings, but I see it like this: the energy of the item is what is being offered to the gods, and after an allotted amount of time, that energy exchange has happened. Disposing of the offering, even in a garbage can, is just disposing of the shell of the item and does not have any disrespect attached to it. But if you wish to dispose of offerings in another way, there isn't anything wrong with that.

Protocol is very important when working with one of the orisha. Perhaps this is because their worship never really died out and has remained in one form or another even in Christian times and remains today. They seem to like what is traditional, unless they nudge you otherwise, perhaps because they are used to being offered these particular things. Gods have memories too after all.

··············

Oya Invocation

I feel you in the wind

In the power behind the storm

Mighty Oya

Fierce Warrior

The wind comes to your call

The thunder echoes your laugher

The lightning is your machete as it flashes across the sky

Mother of Nine

She who brings change

Help me clear away

All that is not needed

Graveyard Dirt

In Santería and Hoodoo graveyard dirt is used for a variety of reasons, such as protection, healing, cursing, breaking curses, banishing unwanted people or spirits, and winning legal battles. Dirt from different types of graves is thought to be good to use in different types of magick. For example, dirt from a child's grave is thought to be powerful for good works, that of the elderly who lived a long, happy life to bring wisdom, a soldier or police officer's for protection, a doctor's for healing. Dirt from specific places can have certain qualities: for example, dirt from a racetrack brings luck in gambling, and dirt from a courthouse brings success in legal battles.[30] Dirt from the entrance of a graveyard is thought to be particularly good for banishing unwelcomed spirits. We can work with Oya, a guardian of the entrance of the graveyard, for gathering and creating graveyard dirt.

When I gather graveyard dirt, I first spend some time at the entrance of the graveyard. I leave nine pennies for Oya and offerings of rum. A quick pour from a flask is good for this, especially if there are other people going in and out of the area who may

---

30. Stephanie Rose Bird, *Sticks, Stones, Roots & Bones: Hoodoo, Mojo & Conjuring with Herbs* (St. Paul: Llewellyn Publications, 2004), pp. 114–15.

be curious about what you are doing. I mentally ask permission to enter the area for the purpose of gathering dirt and honoring the dead. At times I will get a negative feeling, unease, or other emotions that signal it's either not a good time or this is not a place I should be taking earth from. If you get that feeling, listen to it and go. When I feel the offering has been accepted, only then do I enter. A breeze or gust of wind can be taken as a favorable response from Oya. Spend some time walking and talking to the spirits here. Leave more pennies and rum at any place you take dirt from, and only if you feel you have permission to do so. When you leave, give another offering of rum to Oya at the entrance. It is also thought that it is a good idea to make at least three stops before returning home and to take a different route home than the way you came, in order to confuse any spirits who may have tried to follow you.[31]

Once you have obtained your dirt, keep it in a sealed jar or bottle. You can mix your dirt with herbs if you wish or add it to other mixtures when you are ready to use it. Mullein is also connected to Oya, and you can mix some of this crushed herb in with the dirt as well.

....
Oya Powder

Use this powder to call on Oya in any kind of battle or struggle. Graveyard dirt can be used in this, but to overcome battles I like to use dirt collected from a courthouse if possible. Leaving offerings to Oya when you collect it is also a good idea.

You Will Need:
Mullein
Graveyard dirt (or dirt collected from a courthouse)
Juniper berries
Magnolia leaves (bay can be substituted)
Salt

Mix all the ingredients in a bowl, and then hold your hands over it, seeing Oya as a whirling tornado. Say,

---

31. Denise Alvarado, *Voodoo Hoodoo Spellbook* (San Francisco: Red Wheel, 2011), p. 223.

Oya!
Storms come at your call
Whirling, fierce warriors
Bring me victory
Oya!
Lady of the winds and storms
Oya, aid me in my own battles!

Store the mixture in a jar until you need to use it.

....

Oya Protection Talisman

Magnolia cones (the seed pods shed from the tree like a pine cone) are thought to have protective qualities. It is thought you can put them under the bed to attract love as well. Tied with red thread along the stem, they can be used as a protective charm for a home. If you are from the South where the tree grows, you are more than likely familiar with these cones, though if you live in the North, you may want to substitute another item for the cones if you cannot locate one from a store or purchase one online.

You Will Need:

Dragon's blood oil

Purple or dark-colored candle

Oya powder

Magnolia cone

Paper plate or newspaper

Red string

Rub a few drops of the oil on the candle. I like to use dragon's blood oil for extra energy in protection work, but you can substitute another oil if you wish. Make sure the candle is covered, and then roll it in the Oya powder. Light the candle on Oya's altar and leave an offering to her, asking her to protect your home. Leave the candle on the altar and light it for a few minutes each night for nine days. When you are ready, on the ninth day take the candle from the altar, light what is left, and drip it on the magnolia cone. Be sure to do this over a paper plate or some newspaper to avoid a mess. Move the cone around so that wax covers the whole surface with a light layer. Set it down to dry. Wrap the stem of the cone with red string or fabric and hang near the doorway of your home.

....

Spell to Oya for Protection against Storms

You Will Need:

Rum

9 pennies

You can burn a candle if you wish but do not need to do so. I might do this before I travel, when I'm traveling and there is bad weather, or when a particularly bad storm is on its way. Pour the rum in an offering bowl or vessel you have designated for Oya. Before you pour it, taste a tiny bit of it, signifying you have made sure the offering is good enough for the gods and not bad in any way.

See Oya standing before you. See her holding her hands up to the storm; where her hands move, the winds move. She controls the storm. Say,

Oya! Lady of the winds!
Lady of the storm, hear me!

See the storm clearly in your head. I like to visualize a weather map, like the ones you would see on the news, and imagine the storm either dissipating into nothing or moving in another direction away from me. Hold that image of it moving or dissolving clearly in your mind. Say,

Oya!
Move the winds!
They still and calm at your command
They blow away from me and mine at your command
I am safe from the storm
Those I love are safe from the storm
It is no more
She who tears

Tear the storm apart!
It is no more!

End with moving your hands in a cutting motion, seeing Oya ripping apart the energy and power fueling the storm.

Leave Oya the nine pennies as an offering.

10

KALI

You find yourself on a wide, parched plain. All around you the ground is dry and split where the dirt is particularly hard and devoid of water. Sparse trees dot the landscape here and there, their branches dried and bare. There are others with you, though you do not have time to look to see who they are. All you know is you are tired to the bone, and you are losing. A battle is being fought. You and the people around you take turns rushing and then backing safely away from a horrible creature that stands defiantly in the center of the wasteland. It is a demon, its skin red as fire, its eyes sunken and fangs protruding from its mouth like tusks.

It is your turn to rush the creature, and you take a few hurried steps forward with your sword raised. The demon seems to sense how unsure you are of yourself and laughs at you, taunting you to strike at it. And you do, sword extended before you, take an angry swing at the creature. You, like the others, are only willing to get close enough to wound one of the demon's many limbs, but not close enough to deliver a deathblow. It laughs again when the sword slices through an arm and a long line of blood stains the ground. You back away to where the others circle, knowing what will happen next. The blood no sooner hits the ground than it begins to transform. It bubbles and steams, and figures soon begin to grow and grow from each droplet of blood. The new demons waste no time in attacking you and the others who fight with you. You fight alongside the others until the new demons lay lifeless on the ground. Their blood may not spawn more of their own kind, but the great red-skinned creature before you will. You are not sure how many times you or the others have wounded him, but no matter how many cuts you make, you are worn down by the attack of the creatures spawned by it. If only someone would dare to strike without hesitation, then perhaps a true deathblow would destroy the creature. But neither you nor the others with you *are willing to risk how many demons would be unleashed with such a deep bloody blow. Keeping the demon surrounded and at bay is all you can hope for it seems.*

Another steps forward and delivers another slash across an arm, and the cycle continues. But this time the red-skinned demon does not stand still, content to watch as the smaller demons attack. Perhaps it has become bored, or maybe it was playing with you the entire time. Whatever the reason, the demon begins to attack the others who have been helping you with ruthless abandon. And you realize that soon you will be standing alone, that this creature has just been toying with you and will annihilate everything you care about.

Fear begins to change into anger, a bright fury that rises up from the very soles of your feet and begins to fill you. This ends here. This ends now. No more fighting and then backing down. No more mercy or compromises. You will win this time. Because there are no more alternatives. You will win, because you have to. Somehow this certainty negates all the fears you had before. And you realize it has not been the fear of the demon that has been holding you back, but your fear of losing and what it would cost you. Now there is no choice left. You must succeed at any cost, or you will lose everything. And there is something liberating about that thought. No more holding back.

As you think that, you feel your very skin ripping and pulling away. It is not painful, but it is as if that swelling, brilliant, defiant rage has taken on a life of its own. And it is too large to be contained by your own form. The old you slides off you like a snake shedding a skin, and you find you begin to grow and grow. You have many arms, all holding weapons, and your skin is as black as the night sky. The rage swells up within you but it comes pouring out of your mouth as laughter.

This makes the demon pause and look in your direction. You do not hesitate as you did before. Lightning fast, you are upon the demon, swords and many arms slashing and fighting with a force of determination you have never felt before. And you see the slightest bit of fear in the demon's eyes. Drops of his blood flow to the ground, but you continue to fight both him and the smaller demons that his blood summons. Then suddenly you know how you can beat him.

You bend your head down, almost as if you embrace the demon or kiss it. But instead you sink your teeth into the skin of his neck. It screams for the first time, trying to get away from you. But you hold the demon close, your many arms embracing it in a macabre hug. And you drink and you drink. You drink in the demon's blood and with it its power. It grows smaller and smaller as you do so, until you drink the last drop and it vanishes.

The demon defeated and gone, you begin to dance and stomp the ground in a wild, mad dance. But soon you feel the shape of your old self returning. The skin you shed before battling the demon comes back around you. You blink, looking at your hands and finding yourself back to normal, but before you still stands the black-skinned, tall, many-armed being that your rage summoned forth. She looks at you and smiles. She is naked save for a garland of skulls around her neck. Her skin is as black as the night sky devoid of stars, and her lips are crimson red, still stained with the blood of the demon. She is awe-inspiring, terrifying, and beautiful at the same time. And you realize that the power you called forth was something divine. The spark that ignited in you called forth Kali, just as Durga and others have summoned the fierce goddess from the depth of their souls.

"I am destruction, I am release. I am joyful and terrible in my dance, for I am without fear. I have no bridle holding me back from doing what is necessary. When we allow fear to rule our hearts, we cripple our ability to achieve our goals. Fear of action prevents action. We fight with one hand tied behind our backs and wonder why we fail. Do not fear. Let your rage and will fill you, and I will come."

She begins to dance, and as she does, the carnage around you begins to change. The barren landscape begins to grow green and lush again and all traces of the demon vanish.

"Do not limit yourself, do not hold back. Dance and rage, and I will dance with you."

Kali inspires both terror and awe. She is portrayed holding a severed head in one hand, a sword in another, and her tongue sticking out dripping with blood. She wears a leopard skin with the severed arms of her enemies as a skirt, and destroys demons the other gods cannot vanquish. In some depictions her skin is ink black, her face and eyes sunken, and body gaunt. *Kālī* means "dark-colored" and is related to *kāla*, meaning "time" in Sanskrit.[32] Given her connection to death, battlefields, and the cremation ground, she becomes the inevitability of time, the one thing no one can escape.

In the Hindu tradition the earliest references to Kali come from the sixth century CE, where she is associated with battlefields as well as the fringes of Hindu society. In Southern

---

32. Thomas B. Coburn, *Devī-Māhātmya: The Crystallization of the Goddess Tradition* (Delhi: Motilal Banarsidass, 2002), p. 108.

India there is a story told about how Kali terrorized a wood, and the people asked Shiva to protect them. Shiva began to dance and the two engaged in a dance contest, which Shiva won. This could possibly represent Shiva's dominance over a local goddess cult. Later in the eighth century Kali is identified with Shiva's consort Parvati. In one story Shiva calls her *Kali* ("the black one") because of her dark complexion. Upset over this, Parvati undertakes austerities in order to get rid of her dark complexion. The dark "sheath" she sheds turns into Kali, while Parvati is renamed *Gauri* ("golden one"). Kali is better known as springing forth into existence from the forehead of the goddess Durga, being a manifestation of her divine wrath. The myth of her springing from Durga's forehead may have been an attempt to integrate one form of the goddess with another. As different sects evolved they may have tried to attract these devotees by associating Kali and Durga with their sects. In both stories Kali emerges from another goddess, hinting that her power is something within us all, waiting for the right moment to emerge.

While Kali has many epithets, the most telling about her nature is *Kālī Mā*, *Mā* meaning "mother." She drinks blood, and more than any other aspect of the Divine Feminine in Hinduism, she stands up and refuses to be ignored. Yet she is still a mother: scholars note, "Whatever her appearance, Kali's devotees look to her as a Mother. She enables them to face up to their innermost fears of death and disorder and by overcoming their fears they progress further on the path."[33] While two of her four hands (at times she has as many as eighteen) hold weapons, one is usually held out, palm up, in a gesture of blessing while the other forms the mudra "fear not."

As the divine personification of Durga's wrath, Kali is essential to killing one demon in particular. When the demon Raktabija was wounded, his blood created more demons. Although Durga and the other gods had no trouble wounding him, they were soon overwhelmed fighting the demons spawned from their efforts. The tale is included in the *Devī-Māhātmya* in verses 8.57–60:

> Then Kali drank Raktabija's blood with her mouth....

---

33. Lynn Foulston and Stuart Abbott, *Hindu Goddesses: Beliefs and Practices* (Eastbourne, UK: Sussex Academic Press, 2009), p. 39.

The blow of his club caused her not even the slightest pain. And from his stricken body wherever blood flowed copiously, there Camunda [Kali] swallowed it with her mouth. The Camunda devoured those great asuras who sprang up from the flow of blood in her mouth, and drank his (Raktabija's) blood.[34]

Kali became drunk on the demon's blood and began a mad killing dance. There are various versions of how Shiva was able to calm her. In one Shiva lay prone on the battlefield until she stepped on him. When she danced upon him, she recognized him as her husband and her madness ceased. In another version Shiva transformed into a child, snapping her out of her bloodlust at the sound of his cries, and she picked up the child to comfort it.

Similarly, there is a story of a band of thieves whose leader wanted to make a saintly monk a human sacrifice to Kali. When he brought the monk before a statue of the goddess, it began to burn, and the goddess emerged from the statue, killing the thieves and drinking their blood while sparing the monk. In both stories Kali is the destroyer of evil, taking quick action against those who threaten the stability of order. They also point to her fondness of drinking blood and being offered it by her followers.

Divine Rage

Kali, more than any other aspect of the Divine Feminine within Hinduism, personifies power and rage. She is at times gaunt, her eyes sunken in, blood covering her tongue. Yet she still glories in the inevitability of the destruction she brings with her, unashamed of her fierce appearance. The rage she unleashes on the battlefield is without equal among the gods, and it is only she who can defeat the demons they fail to slay. Despite all the bloodlust, and her madness from drinking demon's blood, she is still a mother, her destruction ending when she hears a child's cry. While we tend to think of rage and anger or really any show of force to be a negative thing, Kali shows us that sometimes rage can be divine. Sometimes it is needed to win our battles.

We are taught to keep our emotions in check. For women, expressing anger is frowned upon and usually chalked up to being a "bitch" or being unfeminine. Unless it

---

34. Ibid., p. 36.

is an emotion that is within the realm of "nurturing," it is often unacceptable. On the other end of the spectrum, men are taught to show no emotions at all, which can be just as harmful and unrealistic. We are all human. We all have emotions that run the gambit from love, rage, hate, and happiness to everything in between. Kali's untamable abandon in all she does reminds us that femininity is not limited to passive emotions. She is rage, battle, and destruction. She is divine rage.

That rage can be a healthy emotion, a divine one even, can be difficult to embrace. Some of my first magickal teachers always stressed that magick should never be done when you felt angry, that you were off center in such a state. Every situation is different, but when you have a real reason to be angry, when you are truly pissed off, there isn't a moment that you aren't more completely in your skin and powerfully focused on a goal. It's in those moments that our focus is razor sharp; our will has a force behind it as strong as Kali's blade. It is also not the kind of anger that blinds us from thinking critically or rationally. Kali is born from Durga's divine rage, her wrath that knows that only through unleashing that most destructive part of herself can she save all that she loves.

In many ways the demon Raktabija represents our fears. In life we are always told to hold back. In martial arts one of the most difficult things to teach a student is to hit without holding back. We are conditioned to only go so far when it comes to our own destructive abilities, and this follows through in other things in life. Our fears make us hold back. When it's really time to fight, our sense of morals, civility, or simply the idea that we must keep our emotions in check makes us hold our true power back. Like the gods who are willing to wound Raktabija but not to deal a death blow, we often face our fears only so much before backing off, only to find that the problem, like the demon who spawns more of his own kind when wounded, has grown tenfold. While the gods hold back, Kali is not chained by such restrictions. She knows you cannot win unless you commit to total war, an unfettered commitment of overcoming the obstacle at hand. Kali does not just wound the demon as the gods do—she has the audacity to consume his blood. Without hesitation, she does whatever is needed to reach her goal, knowing that it's not a matter of if she will win but when. She is time, after all. All things must succumb to her. Kali takes the power out of fear, symbolized here by drinking the demon's blood. She takes the fear within herself and uses it to give herself the strength to overcome it.

Our own fears are no less paralyzing than Raktabija is to the gods. If we face them without holding back, if we unleash the divine force, the divine rage within us, to overcome them, then like Kali we become unstoppable. David Kinsley describes Kali's untamable nature as a lesson that reminds us that the world is not always as orderly and civil as we think: "Kali puts the order of dharma in perspective, perhaps puts it in its place, by reminding Hindus that certain aspects of reality are untamable, unpurifiable, unpredictable, and always a threat to society's feeble attempts to order what is essentially disorderly: life itself."[35] Sometimes our inhibitions, the fears that hold us back, keep us from making breakthroughs. We think that the world is supposed to be orderly and that we must make ourselves fit into certain boxes and roles. We forget that parts of ourselves are as untamable as Kali and that it is those parts of our souls that when unchained lead us to our biggest breakthroughs.

Devotional Work and Offerings for Kali

When I do devotional work with Kali, I often offer her things that are red or black. For offerings that involve moving past my own self-made limitations, I will use a lancet to prick my finger and offer her my own blood, usually by anointing the statue or her image with it. Red wine or dark red juice, reminiscent of the color of blood, are other offerings I use, as well as red flowers.

If Kali had a motto, I'd like to think it would be *Aut viam inveniam aut faciam*, Latin for "I shall either find a way or make one." Supposedly, this was Hannibal's response when his generals told him that it was impossible to cross the Alps by elephant. Kali has that kind of resolve. She will find a way or make one with an earth-shattering dance of destruction. When she wishes to accomplish something, she does it devoid of fear. Call on her to shed fear and spark determinations within. After I make offerings to her and sometimes when I do meditation or journey work with Kali, I will sit with my hands making the mudra gestures she is often shown doing in Indian artwork. One hand I hold at waist level to the side, palm facing upward, symbolizing blessings. It looks very much like holding your hand out with your fingers together and flat for someone to place

---

35. David Kinsley, *Hindu Goddesses: Visions of the Divine Feminine in the Hindu Religious Tradition* (Los Angeles: University of California Press, 1988), p. 129.

something in that hand. The other hand I hold in the mudra for "fear not," hand upward at about shoulder height with the index finger touching the thumb to form a circle.

....

Invocation to Kali

Kali

Shyama, dark one

You dance untamed

You dance through madness

You dance with resolve

Unrelenting time

Uncompromising when faced with a goal

Kali

Lend me your wildness

Let me dance unchained

Let me be without restraint in my battles

That I may drink my own fear

Like honey wine

And be the stronger for it

Kali, dance with me

Kali, be one with me

....

A Song Poem to Kali

BY IVY NEEL

O fierce Kali, O Dark Mother

I feel the pulse of every beat in this world

With your blood-red tongue

And demon-skulled necklace

You showed me what it is

To know every breath in this world

O great goddess, O Kali, O Kali, O Kali Ma

You are beyond time

O Dark Mother primordial
I humbly lay myself down before you
With my eternal gratitude
I promise to bear your arms
I shield myself from the faces of demons
Singing sweetly of desire never-ending
Nectar of temptation full of highs
I walk away and hold these arms up
Heavy on my back, the task is at hand
Slay the demons, and ride home at last

················

Ritual to Kali to Overcome Obstacles

This ritual is simple and can be done in front of an altar to Kali or be incorporated into a full ritual. If you are doing it with a group, choose one person to dance and embody Kali, while the rest of the group can continue to chant, *Kali Ma! Creator, Destroyer, dance, Kali, dance!* and visualize Kali destroying the obstacles that lie before them until the energy has peaked.

You Will Need:

Red flowers (or another offering of choice to Kali)

Red wine (or cranberry juice)

Earthy primal music (optional)

Leave the flowers on Kali's altar as an offering. Then pour some of the wine in a libation bowl or vessel you have for that purpose on her altar. Stand if you are not doing so already, and allow your hips to sway. If you choose to, you can play music in the background during your ritual; something earthy and primal works well. Allow yourself to dance, seeing yourself transforming into Kali. It does not have to be choreographed but can be stomping primal movements. See the fierceness of Kali flowing through you with each movement until you are humming with power. Say these or similar words:

Kali,

Dark one

Mother of destruction

Mother of mankind

Dance with me, Kali

Dance with abandon

And trample all that lies

Between myself and my goals

Be the fire that burns clean the ground

To make way for new growth

Burn bright burn strong, Mother Kali!

See yourself crushing your obstacles beneath your feet. They shatter and are powerless and insignificant in the wake of Kali and yourself. When you feel the energy has reached a peak and you have put enough energy into destroying the obstacles before you, slow your dance and become still before that altar. Say,

Kali Ma!

Creator, Destroyer

Dance, Kali, dance

The obstacles that lie before me are trampled down

Let it be so, Mother!

Pour some more wine for Kali as an offering.

....

Kali Invocation Welcoming Ritual

BY IVY NEEL

This is a simple but effective way that I like to open a ritual or make an offering to Kali. In this case, you are inviting Kali into your home and honoring her presence.

You Will Need:

Small bowl of milk

Red hibiscus (optional; you may also substitute an image of the flower or use a different red flower)

Sandalwood or Nag Champa incense (or any incense you like)

Image or statue of Kali (substitute a red candle or a Kali candle if neither is available)

Gather the small bowl of milk, the flower, and incense in front of the Kali statute or image. If you are using a red candle to represent Kali, light it now. To begin, ground and center for a few minutes. Then light the incense. At this time, close your eyes briefly and take a few deep breaths. While you're breathing, allow yourself to see her image. As the image becomes clearer and clearer to you, chant out loud or silently to Kali. You can use *Om Jai Ma, Om Kali Ma* or this, which I like to use sometimes: *O Primordial Goddess, O Dark Mother, O Demon Slayer, O Great Kali, I honor you.*

Once you feel ready, open your eyes and offer Kali the bowl of milk and the red hibiscus in your own words, and then put your hands together in a namaste as you ask for Kali's blessings. Extinguish the red candle or incense. Leave the milk offering as long as you wish for the day. I left mine overnight before offering it back to the earth the next day. Offer the flower to the earth the next day also if used.

11

ERIS

You find yourself on the stone steps of a great temple. The steps are smooth, polished marble, as are the pillars that frame the temple's wall. The stone of the temple seems white at first, but you notice it has veins of black running through the stone. At the temple's doorway there is a basin of water held up on a metal tripod, and you bow your head and wash your face and hands before you enter into the temple itself.

As you step inside you are immediately greeted with plumes of incense wafting through the air. The inner temple is dark, almost giving the illusion that the smoke is rising from the floor and the black veins of marble in it. There are murmured voices in the dark corners of the temple, and you know there are other devotees leaving offerings and making petitions to the goddess who calls this temple home. Their words are muffled, and despite being aware of their presence, you feel as if you have the temple to yourself.

As you walk deeper and deeper into the temple, past elaborate pillars, you become aware of an altar in an alcove to one side. You are unsure why you did not notice it before. There is a metal brazier burning with sweet-smelling incense. On the wall is a beautiful painting of a goddess. On the walls beside the altar are scenes of war and conflict mingled with scenes of competition. The goddess herself looms above the scenes, large wings on her back. Her hair is wild, a dagger in her hand, and she flies above the chaos. Her shoes have wings as well, and her clothes are torn in some places, yet she has an almost blissful expression on her face. Below the artwork, a crimson cloth drapes over a stone diadem with a single item upon it. It is unclear if the apple is an offering left by another devotee or something else entirely. Stepping closer, you see it is made of solid gold, yet it is so lifelike you were at first glance fooled into thinking it was a real apple. Entranced, you bend closer and admire the craftsmanship of the thing. On it there are letters, though not in *a language you recognize. You pick up the golden apple and trace your fingers over the letters. Tē kallistē, it says, "to the fairest." And suddenly you think of all the reasons that does not describe you, although you wish it did. You think of why others have not deemed you to be good enough and the mix of feelings that comes with it. You both believe it must be true and rebel at the same time, wishing it were not. Why should you not have this apple? Why is anyone else worthy and not you?*

The wave of jealousy and emotions is heady, but it passes just as quickly as it came over you. You straighten up, no longer holding the apple possessively. You look at it once more, still beautiful, and set it down once again on the altar. With a deep breath, you look at it and the image of the winged goddess above it and say, "I am enough. Just as I am." And the last dregs of that heavy wanting feeling are washed away.

Someone places a hand on you. Startled, you turn and meet the dark eyes of a woman. Her hair is loose and flowing with a few strands braided and pinned around her head. She wears flowing robes of black and red with regal golden fringes. Her lips are red like wine and turn up in a knowing and somewhat mischievous smirk. "Not everyone can resist the apple," she says. She scoops it up off the altar, playfully tossing it from hand to hand. "All of life is about wanting and desire." Her voice is silky, and the smoke from the incense in the temple swirls around her like phantom wings.

"What we do with desire matters. We live on the very edge of a blade. Can we walk it without faltering? Or will our desires turn to jealousy? Instead of striving to be better, to carve out our own desires from the world, will we always think that what someone else has is better? That what someone else thinks is more important than what we think?" She smiles and extends out the apple, offering it to you. "We are all the fairest. That is the secret. The trouble is we forget that the only person we should let judge our worth is ourselves. Craving the judgment of others will not make us the fairest—it will only quiet the fear in the pit of our stomachs that says, 'You are not worthy.' It is the poison that twists our drive in life to jealousy."

She welcomes you to take the apple, and you do. The form of the woman, who you know must be Eris herself, begins to become less substantial. As if she is fading into the dark and smoke as she speaks. "I challenge you to know your own worth. And if you don't, I'll be there to break down every wall, to tumble you into chaos and strife until you know it deep in your heart. The heart that has never known strife has no true measure of its worth or the worth of others. Know your own full measure, and do not mourn the chaos that gave you the fullness of that wisdom. Celebrate it for what it is. Knowledge, even the most painful kind, is greater in worth than any gold."

And with her words, she fades in the darkness. The temple begins to fade as well. All that is left in your vision is the shining golden apple in your hands.

Eris is the Greek goddess of strife, daughter of Zeus and Hera, though she is alternatively named the daughter of Nyx. In ancient depictions Eris is shown with wings, her unbound hair flowing from her head, a dagger in hand, and often in torn clothes. She is sister to Ares, the god of war, and Homer equated her to the war goddess Enyo, perhaps because she often accompanied her brother in his chariot. In *The Iliad* Homer tells us that Eris's "wrath is relentless, she the sister and companion of murderous Ares, she who is only a little thing at the first, but thereafter grows until she strides on the earth with her head striking heaven. She then hurled down bitterness equally between both sides as she walked through the onslaught making men's pain heavier."[36]

She is attributed by Hesiod to be the mother of most of the less desirable traits of humanity, with the exception of Oath:

> And hateful Eris bore agonizing Toil,
> Forgetfulness, Famine, and tearful Pains,
> Battles and Fights, Murders and Manslaughters,
> Lawlessness and Recklessness, who share one nature,
> And Oath, who most troubles men upon Earth
> When anyone willfully swears a false oath."[37]

While the last trait, Oath, sounds harmless, noble at times even, Eris perhaps reminds us that false oaths are often given and that many break their oaths no matter their intent when they first gave them.

---

36. Homer, *The Iliad of Homer,* book 5, lines 440–45.

37. Hesiod, *Works & Days; Theogony,* trans. Stanley Lombardo (Indianapolis, IN: Hackett Publishing, 1993), lines 226–32.

Eris is perhaps best known for her role in causing the Trojan War. When the gods were invited to the wedding of Peleus and sea nymph Thetis (who would later be the mother of Achilles), Eris was not invited, most likely due to the troublesome spheres she held sway over. Not to be slighted or ignored, she tossed a golden apple inscribed with *Tē kallistē,* or "to the fairest," into the area in which the guests gathered. Hera, Athena, and Aphrodite all claimed it was meant for themselves. Zeus, not wishing to judge who was the fairest among them and end the quarrel, appointed the mortal Paris to choose among the goddesses. Each promised him a different reward for choosing her, and in the end Paris found Aphrodite's offer of the most beautiful woman in the world to be the most tempting. The discord continued after Aphrodite was named the fairest, as Helen, the most beautiful woman in the world, was already married. Paris inadvertently caused a war by claiming his prize. As the events of the Trojan War unfolded, even the gods picked sides, some aiding the Achaeans and others favoring the Trojans. In all senses, mortal and immortal worlds were thrust into conflict and strife.

The story of the apple paints Eris as spiteful and dangerous, yet at the beginning of *Works and Days* Hesiod describes Eris as being dual natured and sometimes useful to mankind: "There was not one kind of Strife alone, but all over the earth there are two.... For one fosters evil war and battle, being cruel.... But the other ... set her in the roots of the earth: and she is far kinder to men. She stirs up even the shiftless to toil; for a man grows eager to work when he considers his neighbour ... and neighbour vies with his neighbour as he hurries after wealth. This Strife is wholesome for men. And potter is angry with potter, and craftsman with craftsman ... and minstrel of minstrel." [38] In this light Eris has a dualistic nature, one side bloodthirsty, inciting the jealousy and battle, while her benevolent side as described by Hesiod inspired healthy rivalry and urged mankind to not be idle. As much as we don't like to admit it, strife is at the very heart of the human experience. It is what allows us to learn and find a will to overcome the obstacles in our path. If we never had any obstacles to begin with, we would never know our own limits or strive to grow. Our trials, our most difficult experiences, shape us. Eris in this light becomes less petty and more of a goddess that rules over a difficult truth. We must suffer to learn, and some lessons can only be learned through pain and hard-

---

38. Evelyn-White, *Homeric Hymns and Homerica,* lines 11–24.

ship. There is also a very competitive side to Eris. The strife that Hesiod describes is the strife that comes from competition. Craftsman against craftsman and minstrel against minstrel in a struggle to hone their craft, to better themselves through the drive created from conflict. Each wanting to be, like the three goddesses, recognized for being the better at something. Anyone who has a competitive nature or who has gone to a sporting event with adamant fans understands how this kind of strife can be a driving force.

The spheres Eris rules over are scary. We don't look forward to having chaos thrown at us, but it is the very thing that sparks changes and teaches us who we really are. Without Eris, we are nothing more than an untested blade. Will we break under pressure or endure? Well, there is only one way to find out.

The emotions Eris rules over are also scary. Jealousy left unchecked, as in the case of the three goddesses competing for the apple, can be destructive. Emotions are messy, and looking at the darker ones is something we don't like to do. But our darker emotions are not things we should hide from or keep at bay. Once mastered, they can be useful tools and are just as much a part of us as the emotions we deem more pleasant.

Eris reminds us that a healthy dissatisfaction with our circumstances can actually be a driving positive force. It can lead us to better ourselves after seeing what someone else has achieved. We know if we work hard and hone our craft we can achieve what the other person has or exceed that. That Hesiod says that there are two Erises signifies that there are two ways strife can drive us. It's our choice.

Devotional Work and Offerings for Eris

My first experiences with Eris were through a coven-mate who was dedicated to both Eris and the Morrigan. Eris had arrived in her life during a time of upheaval, and ironically the goddess of strife helped her mend things in a relationship that had turned stormy. When the group worked together, we would often call on the Morrigan, Hekate, and Eris together, each goddess representing the personal dedication of different people in the group. As much as calling those three together sounds like a bad idea, it all worked quite well. The three balanced each other out in different ways, all having some connection to either strife or being a psychopomp. Eris's energy felt sultry and smoky, perhaps even alluring. She is rather shameless, knowing that her gift can cause a breakthrough or hinder a person. She never felt malicious in my mind. Just because we don't value strife doesn't mean it isn't useful or necessary. She does not cause strife for the sake of chaos—at least not all the time—but rather knows that we need to be shaken up sometimes. We need challenges to overcome lest we remain stagnant.

My own offerings to Eris include rich red wine and apples (preferably yellow ones). When I call on her, I have a small bowl of earth mixed with a few pinches of salt, echoing Hesiod's description of "set her in the roots of the earth," as a reminder that strife can be a useful thing. Eris's nature can inspire either the blood of war to soak into the ground or us to hone our crafts and skills, and that spirit of strife can create a fertile ground for us to grow in. Which direction we take her energy is up to us.

Honoring Eris is a lesson in embracing chaos. The more you try to avoid it the more she will bring it on. Working with Eris demands that we see the good that chaos and strife create in the wake of their upheaval, instead of just seeing them as negative things. Part of Eris's gift is teaching us that we can't control everything. This is a very difficult lesson if you are the type of person who likes to be in control. But Eris reminds us it's a false sense of control. The world is full of chaos, even thrives on it in some cases, and we have to learn to roll with the punches and sudden change if we are to survive. Being adaptable to change and not letting it break us is perhaps the most important thing she can teach us.

As with any deity, be careful what you ask for. Eris's wisdom can be extremely insightful and helpful, but ask her for her chaos and don't expect it to be any less than a hailstorm. Sometimes we need our lives to be stirred up, but be clear about what you ask her for.

....

Invocation to Eris

Lady of Chaos
Harsh Strife
I give you your honored due
Fertile Chaos
Soaking the battlefield
Stirring men's hearts to strive
Sister and companion of Ares
Teach me that struggle is necessary

Teach me to walk on the knife's edge
To dance on the ruins of the old
And welcome the uncertainty of change

....
Ritual to Know Thyself

You Will Need:

Salt

Bowl of water

Incense or other offerings to Eris

Wine (or dark-colored juice)

Apple

Mix a few pinches of the salt in the bowl of water. Use the bowl of water to wash your hands before you begin the ritual and sprinkle some around the area you are working, saying these or similar words:

I wash my hands before seeking the praises of the gods
May all pollution be gone from me

Light the incense and waft the smoke over the altar. Take the glass of wine and hold it over the altar, saying,

Eris, I offer you incense in your honor
I bring you wine and offer it in praise of you

Invoke Eris or simply see her standing before you. Let the image settle firmly in your mind. What does she look like? What color is her hair, her eyes? Does she say anything to you? When you are ready, hold the apple in your hands, saying,

Eris, who tears down the wall
Eris, who is strife
Who challenges us to strive
To know our own passions
May I know the fullness of my worth

May I know the measure of my successes and failures
May I know pain and chaos bring with them wisdom
And understand that can only be felt, not granted
Eris, who holds the apple of discord
May I know
I am the fairest

Cut the apple in half and leave one half as an offering to Eris. Take a bite of the other. Spend some time meditating and speaking with Eris. Ask her to help you see your own worth and know it. Ask her to help you let go of the need for others to see you a certain way or the feeling that their judgment is more important than your own.

....

Spell to Calm Chaos

Sometimes we find ourselves surrounded by chaos. Everything is coming at us at once, from all directions. It is generally believed that a deity that can cause something can also take it away. The Egyptians believed Sekhmet brought pestilence, yet physicians called on her to ward off disease. Likewise, Eris, who is known for causing chaos, can also be called upon for taking it away.

You Will Need:

Red wine

Bowl (optional)

Cast a circle if you wish. Call to Eris and see her standing before you. Pour the red wine as an offering into a bowl or on the ground if you are working in an outdoor space. Say,

You who are the whirlwind and churn the storm
Let the storm quiet to a breeze
Let this chaos return to peace
Eris, I leave you this offering
Turn the tides for me, Eris!

In your mind's eye see a storm churning over your head calm to a summer breeze. See things calming down in your life, and hold that image in your mind until it is perfectly clear. When you are ready, thank Eris.

12

Ereshkigal

You stand at the base of a mountain. Its rises up far into the sky, so high you cannot see its peak. But it is not to see the highs of heaven that you have come to this place. No, you know those heights; you have ruled them, yet what lays below, what dwells in the underworld, is a mystery to you. On your brow is a crown. You touch it for a moment, thinking of what it represents to you. Is it your rank in life? How others see you? Your job? On your wrist is a glistening bracelet, beads and metal entwined with gems. You touch this briefly too and think of the skills it represents to you, the things you are best at and have created with your own hands. You touch the fine fabric you wear. It is intricate and woven with care. You think of what it represents to you, the things you hold closest to yourself, the things you are the proudest of, your achievements. Last, you touch the breastplate you wear over your garment, beautifully hammered and decorated with spiraling images of animals, crafted to be stronger than any blade. All your finery, your symbols of rank and achievement, makes you feel confident you can complete this journey and win the mysteries of this realm.

Carved into the side of the mountain is an enormous stone doorway. It is the first of many gateways you know that lead to your sister's realm. It towers at twice your height, but you feel confident and knock loudly. It is only a few moments before the massive stone door opens inward and a cloaked figure welcomes you, gesturing for you to enter through the door. You enter the darkness still unafraid and bold. But before you get more than a few steps into the dark, the gatekeeper's hand bars your progress.

"What is this?" you ask.

The gatekeeper, without asking, takes the crown from your head. "Quiet. The ways of the underworld are perfect and cannot be questioned."

You do not protest, but you feel just a twinge of unease at the crown's loss. Without your status, what are you? But you continue on into the dark. The passages of this place are made of polished black stone, and if there had been windows, you could imagine yourself in a grand castle. Soon you find yourself at another door like the first one. Another gatekeeper stands before it. You tell the gatekeeper you wish to pass, and without a word the gatekeeper steps forward and takes the bracelet from your arm.

Shocked, you ask, "What is this?"

The gatekeeper motions for you to pass through the stone doorway and says only, "Quiet. The ways of the underworld are perfect and cannot be questioned."

You pass through more rattled now. Without the things you have created, without the things you excel at and your achievements, what are you? But still you go on. You can't give up now.

Soon, as you make your way deeper into the dark, you come to another doorway and another gatekeeper. This gatekeeper too opens the door for you, and you think you will pass without consequence when the gatekeeper reaches out and easily takes the breastplate from you. The straps undo of their own accord.

"What is this?" you ask angrily.

The gatekeeper motions for you to pass through the stone doorway and says only, "Quiet. The ways of the underworld are perfect and cannot be questioned."

You look deeper into the dark, uncertain now. What are you without the armor that protects you? But you must go on. There is no choice.

Traveling deeper and deeper, you come to a final gateway. You know the heart of the underworld must lie behind these doors, and there is nothing else you can possibly give up to the gatekeeper. At least, that is what you think at first. The gatekeeper reaches out, and as he touches your fine clothes, the seams open up at his touch and easily flow to his hands.

Sobbing, you ask, "What is this?"

The gatekeeper motions for you to pass through the stone doorway and says only, "Quiet. The ways of the underworld are perfect and cannot be questioned."

Naked, you walk through the doors. What are you then? you ask yourself. You aren't really sure. You thought you were all the things the gatekeepers stripped you of. If you are not those things, then what lies beneath all of that? What are you? How is it that you remain, can even exist, without those things? Aren't those the things that define you? Make you? You are not sure now.

You walk into the heart of the underworld naked, arms wrapped around yourself. And there you find the sister you sought from this journey's beginning. Ereshkigal, cloaked in dark robes, sits on a throne carved on black stone.

"Do not cower so. Yes, you do not wear your beautiful crown, nor are you protected by your armor or adorned with your fine clothes or gems. But your worth was never weighed by them. The being I see before me is in all its glory unfettered and has more worth naked than hidden and encumbered by all the things you think you are. It is not until we strip away the illusions, the things we tell ourselves that we must be, that we learn what it is that we truly are." *She steps toward you and takes your face in her hands comfortingly.* *"The ways of the underworld are perfect and cannot be questioned. Their perfection is painful and harsh, but when we have survived their trials, we learn our own worth. Stripped bare, we gain this knowledge, and it is something that cannot be taken away from us."*

You think of how you can define yourself without the things that the gatekeepers have taken away from you. You let the shape of that being fill your senses. Without all the things you think you needed, you still exist. Stripped bare of everything, you still exist.

"Remember who you truly are," *Ereshkigal whispers, and you promise yourself you will.*

The Mesopotamian goddess Ereshkigal (Great Lady under Earth) was a goddess of Irkalla, the underworld and land of the dead. Her main temple was located in Kutha, an ancient city whose location would have been in modern-day Iraq. Our earliest record of her stories comes from an offering list dating to the twenty-first century BCE. In the Sumerian creation myth, Ereshkigal was created with her twin brother Enki from the tears of the god An. Although the remains of the story are fragmented, we know that the primordial dragon Kur stole Ereshkigal away to the underworld. What happened next is unclear, only that Enki returned from the underworld with seeds that would produce the Tree of Knowledge and that Ereshkigal retains the underworld as her own realm.

Ereshkigal is best known for her interactions with her sister Inanna (in Babylonian mythology her sister is named Ishtar). In *The Descent of Inanna* the goddess Inanna descends to the underworld, telling her advisors to come retrieve her if she does not return. She told them Enki knew the secrets of the herbs that restored life and that he could return her to life if she died. As she descends through the seven gates of the underworld, Inanna is forced to remove the symbols of her status, until finally she must remove her clothes and stand before her sister naked.

Inanna's reasons for entering the underworld are not always clear. When she meets the first of Ereshkigal's gatekeepers, she tells him she wishes to observe the funeral rites of Ereshkigal's husband, who had just been killed. The details of Gugalanna's death can be found in the *Epic of Gilgamesh*, and while it is not mentioned in *The Descent of Inanna*, it is Inanna's own actions that cause the death of her sister's husband. Yet when she finally reaches the depth of the underworld, she tells Ereshkigal to rise from her throne that Inanna may sit upon it, perceivably wishing to take ownership of both the realm above and the realm below. For her arrogance she is judged and hung from a hook where her corpse begins to rot. When Enki learns of this he laments, "My daughter craved the great heaven and she craved the great below as well.... The divine powers of the Underworld are divine powers which should not be craved, for whoever gets them must remain in the underworld. Who, having got to that place, could then expect to come up again?"[39]

As Inanna had guessed, Enki eventually sends servants into the underworld to find his daughter and give her a concoction that would restore her to life. But Ereshkigal decrees that no one who has died has ever left the underworld and that if Inanna is to return to the world above, she must send someone in her place.

Returning to the world of the living, Inanna passes three of her servants, properly mourning their mistress. Yet when she finds her husband, he is not in mourning at all but instead feasting. She then chooses him to be her replacement in the underworld.

The Descent of Inanna has many layers. Like many myths, there are several lessons you can take from it. On one level Ereshkigal and Inanna are just different sides of the same goddess. Ereshkigal dwells in the underworld, both the shadow and the true self devoid of ego. Inanna is the conscious self, journeying down to the depths to confront her shadow and know her inner self. And when she finally confronts her shadow, she de-

---

39. Jeremy Black, "Inana's descent to the Underworld," in *The Literature of Ancient Sumer*, ed. Jeremy Black, Graham Cunningham, Eleanor Robson, and Gábor Zólyomi, (Oxford: Oxford University Press, 2006), p. 71, lines 190–94.

mands her throne, not quite accepting the truth the shadow offers. To reach the throne in the first place, she must shed her illusions by leaving items of status and her clothes at the gates, representing the shedding of the ego. When Inanna is revived and leaves the underworld, she is reminded that part of her still belongs to that realm. Ereshkigal tells her no one ever escapes the underworld, just as no one ever escapes their shadow. Thus, she must send someone in her place, reminding her she will always be tied to that realm in some way even when she leaves it. The illusions she carried with her before her journey are also stripped away when she returns to the world of the living and sees her husband's behavior with new eyes. This interpretation is perhaps the most acknowledged one, but there are other layers of meaning to the story of Ereshkigal and her sister.

The second layer to Ereshkigal's story is that we are all responsible for our actions, and that our actions have consequences. When the hero Gilgamesh rejects the sexual advance of Inanna, in retribution she sends her sister's husband, Gugalanna, to punish the hero. Gugalanna, better known as the Bull of Heaven, could make the earth shake with his feet and drink up entire rivers. But Gilgamesh and his companion Enkidu manage to kill the bull. Enkidu goes as far as to wave a piece of the dismembered bull at Inanna, telling her he would do the same to her if he caught her. Gugalanna's death and subsequent funeral rites are the reason Inanna gives for entering the underworld. It should not be surprising that her sister insists she take responsibility for her actions. In *The Descent of Inanna* we are told Inanna is judged by her sister along with the judges of the underworld and that she let out a cry of guilt. Being judged and hung on the hook then can be seen as paying the price for the death she caused. Her father of course restores her to life and she returns to the world above, but not without the price of sending someone in her place. Justice is served, and as Inanna travels to the underworld willingly, this may show that she planned to be judged by her sister and pay the price in order to make peace. Ereshkigal does not drag her sister to the underworld, although she is powerful enough to do so. In one story when the god of disease insults Ereshkigal by being rude to one of her servants, she has him dragged down to the underworld to explain himself. She does not do so with her sister. Instead she allows Inanna to be the one who chooses to make amends.

Owning Our Actions

Ereshkigal reminds us that to shed our ego and truly know ourselves requires we take ownership of our actions. We are human; we are going to fail at things at times and create messes in life. But how we deal with that fact is important. Do we, like Inanna, travel to Ereshkigal's realm and make amends? If we see the sisters as two sides of the same goddess, can we forgive ourselves for our misdeeds? Perhaps the hardest lesson of all is to forgive ourselves. Can we judge ourselves, know we must act differently in the future, and know we are worthy of that forgiveness? To do so we must sacrifice a part of ourselves, shedding that which hinders our growth as Inanna must shed her clothes and regalia to stand before Ereshkigal's throne. And to be Ereshkigal ourselves we must sit on that throne knowing we must judge ourselves as well. That is the price of escaping the underworld.

Devotional Work and Offerings for Ereshkigal

When I do devotional work with Ereshkigal, I offer her dark-colored wine or a plate of food with the first choices of the meal, as she was shown discourtesy during the feast of the gods. I wear my hair loose and do not wear any jewelry, as a symbolic sign that I come to her gates as I am, without regalia. Ereshkigal is a goddess to call on to move past guilt and to reclaim our shadow, the parts of ourselves that we are ashamed of and shun. She is also a deity to go to when we are mourning a loss or one who has passed. Even as the queen of the underworld she is powerless to prevent her husband's death.

....

Invocation to Ereshkigal

You who sit enthroned in the underworld
You who sit in judgment
You strip us bare
You show us what we truly are
Without finery, raw in the knowledge of ourselves
Ereshkigal, lady of the darkness
May I know myself

May I see the truth of my spirit
As you see it

....

Invocation to Ereshkigal and Inanna

Ereshkigal, Inanna
Dark lady, heaven's queen

May we be stripped bare before you
May we know our true worth

Ereshkigal, Inanna
Dark lady, heaven's queen

That the crowns we wear have no worth
Compared to the mettle of our will

Ereshkigal, Inanna
Dark lady, heaven's queen
Barefoot and bleeding we come to you
Grieving and in sorrow we come to you

Ereshkigal, Inanna
Dark lady, heaven's queen
We lay our sorrows at your feet
We lay our fears at your feet
We lay the crown of heaven at your feet

Ereshkigal, Inanna
Dark lady, heaven's queen
Be here now!

Making Things Right Spell

Sometimes we mess up. We aren't perfect. Sometimes with the best intentions we burn bridges we never intended to set on fire. Owning our actions means when things like this happen, we have to take ownership of what we have done and attempt to fix things. Part of this, of course, has to be done in the practical everyday world, but we can use magick to help us pave the way and help foster the conditions for making a situation right again.

You Will Need:

Small jar

Picture (or item representing the person you wish to make peace with)

Bottle of honey

Take the small jar and put in it a picture or item of the person you want to make amends with. You could also take a piece of paper, write down the situation, and put it in the jar. Pour the honey over the item and fill the jar until it comes close to the lid. Then put the lid back on. Say,

Ereshkigal, I seek to make amends
I have acted wrongly
And take ownership of my actions
Help me make amends
Sweet honey to cool tempers
And open hearts
Help me right the rifts I have made

See the person or situation healing and both parties being open to listening to the other. Leave the jar in a hidden place in your home until the desired results have manifested.

Ritual to Connect with Our True Selves

There are times when we need to let things go or to forgive ourselves before we are able to heal or move on. In this ritual we will enact our own descent and stand before Ereshkigal's throne in order to shed the baggage we hold on to and to see ourselves as we truly are.

To enter Ereshkigal's realm we must, like her sister, stand before her bare. In this ritual we will do this in a figurative sense and strip ourselves of ego and pride, instead of clothing, to reveal our truest selves. You will need four items that represent aspects of your ego and pride. These can be things you create to represent these concepts or actual items, such as a diploma, a pay stub, a name badge from work, a picture of your child, and so on. We tell ourselves we are these things, but we forget that the core of who we are exists without those things and is not defined by them.

You Will Need:

Offering bowl

Red wine (or red juice)

4 items that represent things you are proud of or achievements you have made

In the bowl pour part of the wine as an offering to Ereshkigal, and then invoke her, saying,

> *Ereshkigal, lady of the underworld*
> *I descend to your realm*
> *To see my truest self*
> *I pass through the gates of the underworld*
> *I strip my spirit bare before you*
> *Ereshkigal, hear my call*
> *Ereshkigal, walk with me*
> *That I may stand before your throne*
> *And be renewed!*

Take the items you have gathered or created and place them around the center of your space near the offering bowl. Take some time to consider why these things are important to you or have been. Take one item at a time and walk over to each of the quarters of your sacred space. Hold the item up in that quarter and speak out loud about why this item has importance to you and why you are letting it go. It's not that the thing isn't actually an important part of you, just that you are more than just that thing. Before you go to get another item to leave at another quarter, say,

> *Ereshkigal, I release my ego, I descend to your realm*

When all of the items have been distributed to the quarters, slowly begin walking counterclockwise around the circle. Take slow, deliberate steps and see yourself walking down, down, down into the vast underworld that Ereshkigal rules over, knowing you have shed your symbols of power and ego in order to travel to this place. As you do so, quietly chant *Ereshkigal*. This will be a walking meditation. Take your time, go slowly, and allow your mind to wander and be open to Ereshkigal's presence and wisdom. See yourself standing before her throne. What does she say to you? What wisdom does she offer? See her holding up a large silver mirror and telling you to gaze at your reflection. What do you see? Who are you at the core of your being, stripped of all the things you thought made up yourself and your life?

When you are ready, come to the center of the space, pour another offering to Ereshkigal, and offer her your thanks. Then walk clockwise around the space three times, seeing yourself returning from the underworld.

Part 4
Rebirth

The phoenix must burn to emerge.
—Janet Fitch, *White Oleander*

We tend to think the story is over when the hero emerges from the underworld. When Inanna returns to the world of the living or Frodo returns to the Shire, the tale is done. Life returns to normal because the adventure, the danger, is over. But that isn't true. While we return to our everyday lives, we are fundamentally different. And usually that means we start the long process of reshaping our lives and the world around us to fit the person we have become. After all, the rule of the underworld is that there is no guarantee of who we will be at the end of the process. If we are changed, then the life we once lived may not suit us anymore. What makes rebirth difficult is that we are creating it on the ashes of our old lives or our old selves. There are haunting reminders of our mistakes and the paths we have chosen in the past. It is easy to want to fall back into comfortable old patterns. It is easy once we are past a crisis point to forget the wisdom we sought from the gods during our most trying times. There is a good reason we do not remember our own births. The event is traumatic, and so is rebirth.

Once transformed, the process is not over any more than the hero's journey is over when he or she escapes the underworld. Discovering who we have become takes time. Incorporating lessons the gods have shown us along the way into our lives does not happen overnight. As in Nietzsche's analogy for change, we become the child, learning things with newfound eyes. Reshaping our lives and our inner landscapes is hard. Holding true to the knowledge we gain through surviving dark times is even harder. In the depths of the underworld we are confronted with our own personal demons, but when we return to everyday life we have to learn to live with them.

Admittedly, it took me a long time to come to terms with the idea of a shadow self. It had always been presented in a way that made it feel like some alien force that was supposed to be warring inside me with my conscious self, something akin to Dr. Jekyll and Mr. Hyde, good Spock versus evil bearded Spock, or that point in the video game when the hero has to fight his shadowy mirror image. These of course are extremes of something that is far harder to distinguish from our everyday selves. Conceptually, we may visualize the shadows as separate from ourselves, but in the end they are our very selves. The shadow is the voice in your head that says you aren't good enough or thinks something rude while you put on a smile and say the polite thing. We create our shadows bit by bit with the parts of ourselves we see as unacceptable, through pain that we bury within, and through our desire to have things we tell ourselves we either are not good enough to have or are forbidden to have for a myriad of reasons. The thing is our inner nature always wins. The parts of ourselves that make up our shadows have just as much force of will as the parts that make up the rest of us. If we feed our shadows the idea that we don't deserve to be happy, then guess what? You never will be. Your own will, the same force that fuels your magick, is actively working and being fed the idea that you shouldn't be happy, and then it manifests it. It's a rather insidious kind of thing. Wrapping our arms around our shadows and singing "Kumbaya" isn't going to fix anything. Seeing the shadow as something outside and separate from our everyday self is only a first step to acknowledging its existence. But it's already something that is incorporated into the very fabric of who you are. To work with the shadow we have to be brutally honest with ourselves. What do we really want? The shadow isn't rational, but it doesn't need to be. It's driven by emotions, which is part of what makes it so powerful. What do we really feel, under the politeness, under what is expected of us? What is the truth? And when we discover that, then we must act on it or come to terms with it. Otherwise, we will undermine the things we really want. And no matter how much we tell ourselves we don't want them or can't have them, at the end of the day we have to admit to ourselves that isn't true. You aren't worthy until you decide you are worthy.

In a modern age when we are taught to be polite, not get angry, and not make waves, there is a great value in our shadow, because it is where our most primal feelings are. Deep gut feelings, primal urges, and the will to fight and survive—the very things that see us through difficult times—all live in our shadow. Listening to your intuition is listening to your shadow, that part of yourself that is perhaps more honest than your conscious self and does not second guess. Ultimately, there is nothing to fear within the darkest parts of ourselves if we just turn and face it and actively listen to it. Doing so is what brings us independence and allows us to trust ourselves and our ability to make decisions that will benefit our lives.

The goddesses in this section all rule over independence and transformation, and accepting our shadow. Each in her own way has the ability to teach us to own our own skin. The process of transformation is not over when we leave the underworld behind. The underworld is where we face trials and shed the parts of ourselves that need to be let go of, and when we emerge changed, it is just the beginning. Leaving the underworld is when we have to live the new truths we have discovered, to make them an active, vital part of our lives.

B
BLODEUWEDD

You find yourself walking on a grassy path. It is dusk and the light is quickly fading in the sky. In the distance you hear the cry of an owl. You look up but see nothing. Then it calls out again, this time louder. You look above and see a beautiful owl crying out as it circles above you. It is snowy white with areas of light brown in its feathers.

It cries out once more, and you begin to feel yourself changing. Your body begins to get smaller, and your arms expand until they become wings. Your feet become claws, and when you cry out, it is the cry of an owl that comes out. Eagerly, you flap your wings and glide into the night air. The night is no longer dark but brightly illuminated to your sharp eyes. The other owl swoops next to you and then flies ahead as if leading you somewhere.

You fly for some time, until the trees of the forest give way to glistening water, and you continue to fly onward. The crescent of the moon shines brightly in the sky and illuminates the water. Your eyes can see the ripples and waves as it moves below. Soon you can see the shape of a small island in the water below. It is no more than a small hill or two rising from the water, yet it is covered with lush apple trees, and there is a mound at its summit with a ring of standing stones.

The owl leads you to the stones, and silently, you land on the top of a gray stone. The owl lands in the center of the mound, and as it touches the ground, it changes. Its white feathers become long limbs and pale blond, almost silver, hair. The woman's face is beautiful yet angled in a way that resembles an owl. Her eyes are the same dark color as the owl's, and you are sure they miss nothing. On her brow rests a wreath of woven flowers, almost like a crown. And you know this must be Blodeuwedd—"Flower Face," they called her—created by magick from May flowers. Transformed by the spells of the magician Gwydion and her own husband. A twinge of sadness runs through you. Is she cursed? Is that why she was in owl form? And you think of how sad her story is.

She laughs, and you realize she is able to read your thoughts. "One person's curse is another's freedom," she says. "I was not content living in my cage. I was a wife, a queen, and was admired by many. But I was not happy." She looks out at the forest. "A gilded cage is still a cage, and I longed for freedom. But there are some who would say I threw away a good thing, that I should have been content. I tell you that no one can choose your own happiness but you. No one but you can know the shape of it, even when others insist they know better than yourself. Hold true to what will fulfill you, and you will always have your freedom"

You think then of what parts of your own happiness you have given up for others or have neglected. You speak with Blodeuwedd and ask her to help you reclaim them. You listen as the goddess gives you some parting wisdom and you know whenever you need her guidance you can return to this place.

Not realizing you have spent the whole night on the isle you see the sun rising in the distance, and as the first rays of dawn touch you, you begin to change back into your own self, and as you do the isle fades away.

Throughout her stories Blodeuwedd must not only fight to discover who she truly is beyond the definitions of others, but must also undergo transformation and ultimately exile to claim her freedom. Usually portrayed as Lleu Llaw Gyffes's plotting, unfaithful wife, Blodeuwedd reminds us to hold true to our own selves.

Blodeuwedd is not born so much as created by the magic of Math and Gwydion, both central figures in the fourth branch of the Welsh Mabinogi. From flowers the magicians create a beautiful woman for a singular purpose, to be the wife of the hero Lleu Llaw Gyffes: "The flowers of the oak, and the flowers of the broom, and the flowers of the meadowsweet, and from those they conjured up the fairest and most beautiful maiden anyone had ever seen. And they baptized her in the way that they did at that time, and named her Blodeuwedd." [40] Lleu's own birth is rather magical, and his mother,

---

40. Sioned Davies, trans., *The Mabinogion* (Oxford: Oxford University Press, 2007), p. 58.

Arianrod, refuses to recognize him. As a consequence, Gwydion raises the boy and goes about tricking his mother into giving him both a name and weapons. Angered at being tricked, Arianrod curses Lleu to never have a wife born on the earth. Gwydion again thwarts Arianrod by using her words against her, instead creating Lleu a wife out of flowers.

From the very beginning Blodeuwedd is never given a choice. She is thrust into a role someone else has crafted for her, not caring if she wished to fill it or not. At first all seems well. Lleu has overcome all the obstacles his divine mother had put in his path, and Math and Gwydion have shown their cunning. But what no one seems to anticipate is that Blodeuwedd soon grows unhappy with the cage others have placed around her. She meets the hunter Gronw Pebyr in the woods and takes him as her lover while her husband is away. And soon the lovers conspire to win Blodeuwedd's freedom from her imposed marriage by killing Lleu. This does pose a problem, though, since Lleu could only be killed under certain circumstances: with a thrown spear made over the course of a year and while everyone is attending Sunday mass, and he "cannot be killed in a house, nor outside; neither on a horse nor on foot." [41]

Blodeuwedd eventually convinces Lleu to tell her the one way in which he could be killed. The loophole is rather bizarre: he must stand with one foot on a roofed cauldron of water and another on the back of a goat. Once her lover has created the spear, Blodeuwedd has her husband demonstrate the strange posture. As soon as he does so, Gronw Pebyr, who has been hiding and waiting for the right moment, strikes him with the spear, and Lleu transforms into an eagle. Blodeuwedd and her lover take over Lleu's lands, but Gwydion finds the eagle and turns him back into a human. After nursing Lleu back to health, Gwydion helps Lleu reclaim his lands. When Gwydion confronts Blodeuwedd, he transforms her into an owl as a punishment. He tells her, "You will not dare to show your face ever again in the light of day … and that [will be] because of enmity between you and all [other] birds. It will be in their nature to harass you and despise you wherever they find you." [42]

41. Patrick K. Ford, trans., *The Mabinogi and Other Medieval Welsh Tales* (Berkeley, CA: University of California Press, 1977), p. 105.

42. Will Parker, trans., *The Four Branches of the Mabinogi* (Dublin: Bardic Press, 2007), p. 558.

Blodeuwedd's final transformation is meant to be a punishment, but in many ways it allows her to obtain what she has sought all along, freedom. On a symbolic level it signifies that she herself has changed. She is no longer a naive girl allowing others to create her future. She chooses to love whom she wishes and change the shape of her life, all of which is met with resistance from those who tried to control her in the first place. Math, Gwydion, and even her husband, Lleu, never stop to ask what Blodeuwedd wants. Her role is chosen for her, based on their own needs and desires. When she exerts her own will, she is seen as the villain and punished for it.

When we choose to change and forge a different path, we encounter resistance from multiple sources. There is our own resistance to change, fearing the unknown of how it will change us. Then there is the outside resistance we encounter from others. As with Lleu and Gwydion it may not be in the best interest of those around us for us to change. If we have coddled those closest to us, they may react badly to a newly found sense of independence. If we make choices others disagree with, the price of independence and liberation may well be some burned bridges.

Sovereignty of Self

While Blodeuwedd is not a goddess of sovereignty in the traditional sense, in which we see the goddess wedding the king and conferring the authority to rule to him, she is a perfect example of personal sovereignty. Our concept of sovereignty is very different from that of ancient tribes of Wales or Ireland. Their concept of sovereignty was linked to the will of the land, personified by a goddess, and the king's connection to it. It was more rooted in tribal affairs and the living land itself. The king was granted rulership over the land and its people by the goddess, and if he ruled well, all would prosper. When the king made poor choices, the land suffered and he was usually dethroned by supernatural means. Personal sovereignty has some similarities. Our bodies and very souls, our deeds, are the landscape in which we must learn to rule rightly so that we may flourish.

But how do we rule ourselves rightly? How do we own our very skins? "Own" is the imperative term there. Do you own yourself? Your victories, your mistakes just as equally? Sovereignty is not about standing on our own personal soapbox and making our voices heard simply because we haven't done it before. It's looking at ourselves honestly and still loving ourselves and dedicating ourselves to steering our lives and deeds in the right direction for the person we are.

Sovereignty is a rather important concept for those who work with the Irish or Celtic pantheons and is particularly important in the tradition I am part of. It is a concept that many goddesses embody, but sadly it's also very misunderstood. More often than not when I see people who feel they have been letting others walk all over them and then embrace the concept of sovereignty, they see anyone questioning them or disagreeing with them as an attack on their newfound sovereignty. They think being the loudest person in the room is claiming themselves, simply because they have never allowed themselves to have a voice in the past. This is, rather, an imbalance, a swing in the other direction. Having a voice is important, but sovereignty is not being the loudest person in the room. It's something far subtler. The loudest person in the room is more than likely using the outburst as a way to make them feel powerful, while inside they are probably terrified they are not. Owning our own skins, owning our deeds and actions, owning the whole of ourselves is something we have to claim for ourselves. It requires constant work and acceptance of ourselves. There is a beauty, a power, a treasure deep within each of us. A hidden worth that no one but us may ever see or realize. But the world is always going to hold us up to their own measure and judge us. Sovereignty is knowing the only judge that matters is ourselves. That there is a piece of us that is beyond value, that belongs to no other. And that is the inner compass we need to use to guide us.

Changing like Blodeuwedd from compliant maiden to transformed goddess full of independence is not easy. The transformation is painful and costly, but the cost of not undergoing it is never knowing our true selves. In becoming the owl, she inherits the night. Gwydion in the end of the story makes this sound like a kind of curse, yet we regard owls as symbols of wisdom. They can see in the dark far better than any other bird, just as Blodeuwedd can help us to see the darkest parts of ourselves clearly. As we discussed in the first part of this book, "dark" is a misleading term. We think of the "darkest" parts of ourselves as something bad, that dark inherently means evil and undesirable. In Blodeuwedd's story, the darkness of night that she is banished to and, essentially, the dark and dangerous parts of herself identified by those who wish to control her, are all her innermost desires. She desires to choose her own lover, she desires freedom, and she desires the ability to makes choices in her life. The only thing that makes the desires dangerous in the story, at least in her husband and Gwydion's point of view, is that she acts on them. She listens to her shadow self to win her freedom. And it transforms her. Gwydion sees it as a curse because her desires are at odds with his own, but ultimately Blodeuwedd gets what she wants, freedom. Transforming into the owl, who navigates the night easily, is simply the outward appearance of the transformation that has occurred within, being able to act of her own innermost desires and see them for what they are. Sovereignty requires that we rule over and know how to navigate our innermost selves. Really claiming sovereignty is, like in Blodeuwedd's story, taking those parts of ourselves back.

Devotional Work and Offerings for Blodeuwedd

Flowers and herbs, particularly oak, broom, and meadowsweet, are good offerings to Blodeuwedd. I like to offer her white flowers in particular. In her darker aspects, and calling on her to break free of oppressing situations, I offer her thorns because they remind me of the talons on a bird of prey. I often make offerings to her at twilight, although you do not have to choose a particular time of day to honor her. Twilight is a liminal time, and for me it is a time of transformation, a time to stand between realms, making it appropriate to honor her and her ability to transform us.

Invocation to Blodeuwedd

Created for a purpose not of your choosing
Blodeuwedd, Flower Face, I call to you
Molded into form by the magick of another's desire
You shift and change, unwilling to be what others wish you to be
Blodeuwedd, Flower Face, she-owl
Blodeuwedd, who no man can claim to own
Blodeuwedd, hear me!
Blodeuwedd, teach me to be free!

Blodeuwedd Ritual to Claim Sovereignty

Call on Blodeuwedd when you feel you need to reclaim sovereignty over your own life or aspects of it.

You Will Need:

White candle

Offering to Blodeuwedd

You can incorporate this into a full ritual or place the white candle on your altar and invoke Blodeuwedd. When you feel her presence, light the white candle, saying,

> *Blodeuwedd*
> *Flower Face*
> *Owl who sees clearly in the dark*
> *Let me claim my own darkness and know it has value*
> *That I may be strong and whole*
> *May I be free of the chains of others' expectations*
> *May I know the desire of my own heart*
> *And not turn away from it*
> *May I have your bravery, Blodeuwedd*
> *You who would take your freedom into your own hands*

Take a moment to think about the areas in your life you need to reclaim sovereignty over. What has led you to lose ownership over these areas of your life? When you are ready, say,

> *I am worthy because _____*

List or describe why you are worthy of taking ownership of your life. Feel the full scope and weight of each thing you list; do not rush through them. Recognize them as true as you say them aloud.

Thank Blodeuwedd and leave your offering on the altar or outside. Light the white candle whenever you feel you need a reminder of why you are worthy and of your own sovereignty.

....

Thorn in My Side Spell

Use this spell if there is someone who is hindering your independence or is actively trying to manipulate you. I would point out that someone who simply does not agree with you is not the same as someone hindering you. This instead is for situations when people are actively trying to manipulate our actions and feelings or are working against us in harmful ways.

You can use as many thorns as you like. I live in a place with a lot of bougainvillea, an ornamental vine that happens to have quite a lot of large thorns. It's often planted not only to look nice but also to keep unwanted guests away. It's also an excellent source for thorns for your magickal workings. Rose thorns or the smaller thorns found on briar bushes are also a good place to find thorns to harvest for your magickal practices. If you do not live in an area where you can go into a wild place to harvest thorns, going to a florist or the flower section in your grocery store is a good resource. Some stores sell roses with some of the thorns remaining on the stems. If they do not, sometimes if you ask for discarded stems (my excuse is usually that I am looking for material for a compost pile), they will give you cut stems that may still have thorns on them that you can use.

You Will Need:
Candle
Carving tool
Essential oil of your choice (optional)
Thorns

In your sacred space call on Blodeuwedd in whatever way you wish. On the candle carve the name of the person who is bothering you. Then draw two lines to form a big X over the name. If you wish to anoint your candle with oil, you may do so. Then stick the thorns into the candle, pushing the sharp ends in so they stay embedded in the wax. As you do so, see all the energy, negative thoughts, and actions the person has directed at you returning to them and piercing them as the thorns pierce the wax. As you chant the following, continue to visualize all that has been directed at you returning to the person who sent it and flowing into them. You are simply returning what belongs to them and shielding yourself from its influence. See the energy rushing back to them easily and eagerly, returning to its source. Say,

Claw and beak
And taloned feet
Blodeuwedd, on evil
Havoc wreak
Justice bring
On pale white wings
Prick of thorn
Wax and burn
Your hate I now return

Repeat the chant as many times as you feel you need to. When you feel ready, thank Blodeuwedd. Let the candle burn down and then throw any wax that remains in the garbage.

....

Blodeuwedd Incense

3 tablespoons meadowsweet

1 tablespoon oak leaves

2 tablespoons heather

½ teaspoon cinnamon

9 whole cloves (or ¼ tablespoon ground)

1 teaspoon hawthorn berries

1 tablespoon violets

Pinch of salt

I like to make this incense during the new moon. Once I mix all the ingredients, I leave the herbs in a covered bowl outside or in a windowsill. For three nights or until I can see the barest sliver of the moon in the sky, I spend a few moments holding the bowl and seeing Blodeuwedd sending her blessing into the herbs.

14

SCÁTHACH

You find yourself on a misty moor. The mist is thick and swirls around the landscape. To one side you can see the jagged rocks of a cliff. The sound of the ocean's waves crashing far below and the scent of salt water fill your senses. You walk through the mist for a while until you come to another cliff face. There is no way forward except for a bridge that reaches over a chasm. You look dubiously at the bridge. Ropes make up the sides and arm rails, with wooden planks forming the walkway. The ropes are thick but they look old. You take a few more steps closer to the edge of the bridge and look through the mists to the other side. You can just make out green earth on the other side and the stones of a fort in the distance.

You put one foot on the bridge tentatively. It seems sturdy enough, and, grasping the rope sides, you begin to slowly make your way across. It is not long before you realize that the fort on the other side of the bridge never seems to get any closer. You can see it, and you are certainly moving and making progress along the bridge, yet it seems no closer. You look behind you and you can see you have traveled several yards. The end of the bridge you started on is still there, and you guess you must be halfway across the bridge, yet somehow you seem unable to reach the other side.

You continue on, thinking perhaps the mist has fooled you, this time taking care to pay attention to how many paces you have taken. Yet still when you look up and gaze at the other side of the bridge, it remains distant, no larger in your vision than when you first started. Frustrated, you begin to run, your anger overriding your fear of the bridge's stability. Perhaps if you run fast enough, you can reach the fort. Taking your hands off the bridge's rope you make a mad dash for the other side. You can see your feet stretched out before you, your strides long, your breath labored with the effort of your speed. You glance away from the wood planks for only a moment and see a woman who you swear was not there a moment ago standing directly in your path. You attempt *to slow down but collide with her anyway. You fall back and grab the ropes to steady yourself. The woman is unmoved. She wears leather armor and carries a sword at her side. Her hair is long and all of it is tied in many small, intricate braids. Her boots are old and worn, mud still on them. This is someone who demands an honest day's work from herself and others.*

"Not everyone can reach my school on Dún Scáith. Are you willing to struggle? To persevere? To get up again when you are pushed down into the mud and tired to the bone? Or will you give up, when given just a taste of challenge? What are you made of?" She asks the last question while looking you up and down in appraisal.

The question echoes around in your mind. What are you made of? There have been times you have given up, times you have failed. But you think of the reason you have come to Dún Scáith, to the school where Scáthach dwells and teaches the greatest of heroes. You decide that even those heroes who learned from the great Scáthach failed at times too. Although her challenging words make you want to shout at her that you are worthy, that you won't back down or give up, you realize this is part of learning. You will fail before you can learn to be better at whatever craft you wish to hone.

While your first reaction was to argue with her, you now think better of it and tell her you will not know what you are made of until she has challenged you, and you offer yourself to be honed like a blade and tested, if she will have you.

She smiles, pleased with your answer. "Good. I would teach a mind that is open, one that may be filled, not one of arrogance that is already full. To learn, to train in one's craft, one must begin assuming one knows nothing. Only then can one learn everything. I will challenge you. Keep an open mind, and I will give you my hard-won wisdom." She vanishes as soon as she speaks the last word.

With new resolve you begin to cross the bridge again. This time the fort begins to grow larger, until the stone tower in the mist grows closer and you reach the other side. There Scáthach waits for you, and you know you can return to this place whenever you wish to connect to her and learn from the Shadowy One who taught the greatest of heroes.

Scáthach, whose name means "shadowy one" in Gaelic, was a great warrior woman and teacher in Irish mythology. She ran a school for warriors on the Isle of Skye, which was named for her. She trained many Irish heroes, the most famous of which was the hero Cúchulain. Cúchulain was told that, while he was skilled, "if he went to Scáthach to learn soldierly feats, he would excel the warriors of all Europe."[43] He vowed to find her school or die trying. While her reputation preceded her, Scáthach and her school at Dún Scáith (an actual castle whose ruins remain today on the rocky coast of the Isle of Skye) were rather difficult to find and gain entrance to. The only way to get to the school was by crossing over a bridge that crossed a valley with jagged rocks. The bridge was magickal, and once one reached the center of it, it rose up and threw the person crossing it back in the direction in which they came. Cúchulain overcame this obstacle by leaping across the entire bridge.

Uathach, Scáthach's daughter, taken with the hero's looks, advises him on how to persuade her mother to train him. The instructions from Uathach also show that Scáthach's skills were not limited to warfare but included seeing the future. She tells Cúchulain to "set his sword between [Scáthach's] two breasts, until she gave him his three wishes," including "to teach him without neglect" and "to tell him what that would befall him; for she was also a prophetess."[44]

Scáthach has a rivalry with Aife, a warrior woman of another tribe; however, in some stories they are sisters. When Scáthach's warriors are about to go into battle with Aife's, Scáthach devises a plan to keep the young warrior out of the fighting. She binds Cúchulain and gives him a sleeping potion. Unfortunately, while another man would have slept for an entire day, Cúchulain regains consciousness within an hour due to his semidivine nature, being the son of the god Lugh and a mortal woman. He breaks free of his bonds and joins the rest of the men on the battlefield. Each day he fights bravely, until it is his turn to meet Aife on the battlefield. Before meeting Aife, Cúchulain asks Scáthach what Aife treasures most in the world. She answeres that Aife loves her charioteer and horses most of all. The next day as Aife and the hero battle, he looks behind her and cries out that her charioteer and horses have fallen down the jagged cliff. Aife of course turns to look, and Cúchulain takes his chance to grapple her to ground and forces her to make

---

43. Kuno Meyer, trans., "Wooing of Emer," *Archaeological Review* 1 (1888), p. 233.

44. Ibid., p. 300.

a truce with Scáthach as well as to bear him a son. She agrees to both, and the feud is concluded.

It is from Scáthach that Cúchulain is given the *gae bolga*, a legendary weapon, and he is the only student she taught the secrets of its use. Translator Thomas Kinsella notes that, as described in the *Book of Leinster*, "The *gae bolga* had to be made ready for use on a stream and cast from the fork of the toes. It entered a man's body with a single wound, like a javelin, and then opened into thirty barbs. Only by cutting away the flesh could it be taken from that man's body."[45]

Lady Gregory tells a story of a faery woman named Scáthach in *Gods and Fighting Men* who may or may not be the same warrior woman. Scáthach of the Sídhe encounters the hero Finn and his companions while she is in the shape of a wild pig. The warriors chase the pig to a faery mound where one of the shining ones tells them he will welcome them into the mound to feast if they let the pig go. The faery man uses a rod to tap the pig, who transforms into a beautiful woman, his daughter Scáthach. Finn asks for Scáthach's hand during the feast, and her father agrees. Before the end of the night, Scáthach plays a harp: "One string it had of iron, and one of bronze, and one of silver. And when the iron string would be played, it would set all the hosts of the world crying and ever crying; and when the bright bronze string would be played, it would set them all laughing from the one day to the same hour on the morrow; and when the silver string would be played, all the men of the whole world would fall into a long sleep."[46] Finn, under the influence of the harp, falls asleep, and when he wakes in the morning, he is outside the faery mound, his hosts nowhere to be found. The harp and its abilities sound very similar to the Dagda's harp. This Scáthach is certainly cunning and has magical abilities, not unlike the warrior woman Scáthach. Whether or not the two are the same person is unclear, and I leave it to the reader to decide.

---

45. Thomas Kinsella, trans., *The Táin: Translated from the Irish Epic Táin Bó Cuailnge* (New York: Oxford University Press, 2002), p. 260.

46. Augusta Gregory, trans., *Gods and Fighting Men: The Story of the Tuatha De Danaan and of the Fianna of Ireland* (London: John Murray, 1905), p. 292.

Discipline and the Lady of Skye

Discipline isn't something we talk much about in Paganism. We make jokes about "Pagan Standard Time" and accept that when you put so many Pagans in one place a ritual that was supposed to start at 7 p.m. will probably start at 9 p.m. But magick, devotional practice, and the connection we build with the gods require a hell of a lot of discipline. Taking a few minutes at the end or beginning of the day to leave an offering or do a devotional act at an altar, while we need to get to work, feed the cat, get the kids on the bus, work all day, and so on, actually does end up being a difficult task. Mundane life often interferes with our spiritual lives, and there just doesn't seem to be enough hours in the day.

Scáthach teaches us that we cannot reach our goals without discipline. She is a skilled fighter, but she also uses strategy to reach her goals. Does she bind Cúchulain to keep him from harm? Or does she know it will only make him fight more fiercely to prove himself? Sometimes having discipline and holding true to our goals can be the most difficult part of any battle. When I work with Scáthach, I am reminded to slow down. That I have to start at the beginning. That I can't always launch headlong at my goal but must build up to it slowly. Persistence in the end is what helps us to persevere. Taking the time to meditate or do a daily devotion in front of your altar for five minutes every day may seem like a small gesture. But in the end it will strengthen your connection to the gods, and your ability to get into a magickal headspace for the bigger magickal workings. This can be applied to any aspect of magickal or devotional practice. When we are enacting change in our lives this same principle is necessary to keep us moving forward and not get stuck in old habits or ways of thinking. Ultimately, if we can't discipline ourselves with the small things, then we will fail at the bigger, more important things we attempt. If we can't bring all our abilities into focus on something simple, then there is little hope of keeping it together for a more intricate task, even though we'd just rather skip the small thing and take on the big achievements before we are truly ready. There will be roadblocks along the way, but like Cúchulain we can't let them stop us from achieving our goals.

Perhaps the hardest kind of discipline that Scáthach teaches us is when to walk away. When we spend all our energy and time fighting the unimportant battles, we don't have the mental energy or stamina to fight the hard ones. At one of her workshops at the annual Morrigan's Call Retreat, Morgan Daimler described a similar lesson she learned through working with Macha, another goddess of warfare and strategy, although it rings true for our work with Scáthach as well. She explained, "Choosing our battles doesn't mean that the battles we walk away from don't matter, just that we've realized that a blade only has so many edges, and a person only so much energy to spend." Knowing when to fight can be just as hard as the actual battle. Discernment and knowing where our energies are best put is vital.

Devotional Work and Offerings for Scáthach

It is debatable whether or not Scáthach is a goddess or just a powerful female figure in Irish mythology. Other characters in the Irish Ulster Cycle like Cúchulain and Queen Maeve can be seen either as having divine status that was later demoted to that of a mortal or being allies we can work with as ancestral spirits from that pantheon. Again, the choice is up to the reader. There are good arguments for either viewpoint. My own perspective on Scáthach is that she is something in between and that one can approach her either way.

In my own practices I began honoring Scáthach, along with Maeve and Boudicca, as ancestral spirits. While I have a separate altar for those who have passed into spirit in my family and the ancestors of blood, my altar for Scáthach and Boudicca was one specifically for the heroic ancestral spirits of the Irish pantheon. Whether they actually lived or not or exist only as mortal beings within the mythology, they can be powerful teachers regardless. All three, including Scáthach, have a very real presence and can be called on in magick or to work through difficult times. Scáthach is very much about strategy, learning from mistakes, and not just thinking that we are good enough but knowing in our bones that we are. She is unyielding in her discipline and reminds us that everything is earned.

There are no traditional offerings that I am aware of for Scáthach, so you can use things that you feel called to offer her. I often offer Scotch for liquid offerings. Another type of offering I give her is a modern take on the *Curadmír*, also called the hero or champion's portion. The champion's portion referenced in Irish literature would have been the best cut of meat or the finest part of a meal, offered to a warrior of great renown during a feast. There are many stories that revolve around heroes fighting one another or engaging in contest to prove who is truly worthy of the Curadmír. Classical writers recorded similar customs in their observations on the continental Celtic tribes. In a modern context the Curadmír can be a small portion of an evening meal or what you perceive to be the best portion of it.

·················

Scáthach Invocation

Shadowy One
Scáthach
Skilled at war
And prophecy
Teacher of warriors
Lady of discipline
You test our strength
May I be steadfast in my goals
May I hold fast in my resolve
Grant me the wisdom of discernment
To know when to go to war
And when to yield
Mighty Scáthach
Aid me in my task!

·················

Creating an Ancestral Altar to the Heroic Dead

Like an ancestral altar, one dedicated to the heroic dead will differ depending on the person creating it. It is a place that represents your personal connection to the beings it is dedicated to. I see the heroic dead as being the heroes of myths who are not quite mortal and not quite gods, as well as historical figures who have inspired us. Boudicca was an actual woman who lived and breathed and fought the Romans. But the legends that surround her, the myths and stories that have been shared and inspired people from the time of her death to now, have made her something more than just human, like a Christian saint who was mortal but upon death takes on a kind of mystical quality that is beyond mortal. Are we connecting to the spirit of the actual woman? Or are we connecting to the being created by her legend and the group energy of so many people telling, and retelling, her story? There is no easy answer to that, and we all have to decide for ourselves the nature of the energy we are connecting to. Regardless, honoring these spirits and asking for their aid and wisdom is rewarding.

I like to keep this altar separate from the altar I keep for those who have passed. As on an altar for a deity, I have an offerings bowl and framed pictures of the beings I wish to honor. To bless your altar burn some sage or an incense of your choice over the area. Place your items on the altar. Hold your hands up in welcoming, seeing the beings you wish to connect to taking up residence on your altar or standing beside it. Say these or similar words:

I welcome to this place the heroic dead
You who inspire great deeds
You who have overcome impossible obstacles
I honor you
May I stir the ancestral fires
May I learn from your stories
May you share your wisdom with me
Hail and be welcome

....

Scáthach Spell to Attain a Goal

If you are the kind of person who starts and stops things easily, Scáthach is a good ally to call on to help you stick with a plan. She does not tolerate doing things halfway, so only call on her if you really want to achieve your goal and want help in doing so.

You Will Need:
Candle (color of your choice)
Offering

On the candle write what your goal is. Before you place it on the altar, hold it in your hands. See yourself achieving the goal clearly in your mind. Ask Scáthach to aid you in these or similar words:

Scáthach, mighty teacher
Warrioress who had no equal
Help ignite in me your determination
Lead me to victory
That I may see my task through till its end

Light the candle and let it burn down. Leave Scáthach an offering.

15

PERSEPHONE

It is dusk and you walk through a beautiful field of flowers. The evening air is fragrant, and fireflies glow as they fly lazily through the air. But there is something in the distance that catches your eye. It is the flicker of light, much brighter than the fireflies. You walk across the field and through a few stands of trees until you find the source of the light. Two torches burn on either side of the entrance to a large cave.

You know this place, and you know that the cave leads to the underworld, the realm of Hades. You feared this place once, but you have walked the paths of the underworld before and you are not afraid. You step into the dark, taking one of the torches with you for light.

The tunnel is rough cut stone, and you walk carefully, watching your footfalls so you do not trip. Down and down you walk, deeper and deeper into the earth. And soon you see gems and other glistening stones that twinkle in the walls in the firelight. There are beautiful things in the dark, in the deep parts of the earth. You know this, and you seek to find the most precious thing that dwells in this realm, the goddess who sits on its throne.

Soon the tunnel opens up to a large chamber. There are many paths and tunnels that lead deeper into Hades, but this seems to be its center, where all the paths lead to and away from. In the cavern's center is a large raised area with a throne carved out of polished black stone. On it sits a woman. Her skin almost shines with a light of its own against the darkness. Her black hair frames dark eyes. And on her head is a crown made of iron, its spikes and spirals reaching upward, as severe and sharp as her beauty is soft and lovely. At her side is a man robed in dark clothes and fine jewels, and you know this must be Hades, whom this realm is named after, Persephone's husband. He rests a hand on her shoulder and looks attentively and longingly at her as *shades and spirits approach her throne and she meets with them, passing judgments and offering wisdom.*

You too join the long line of spirits waiting to have an audience with Persephone. And soon you too stand before her. You ask the question you have come to ask, and listen as she speaks to you.

When you are ready, you rise from your kneeling position before her throne and turn to go. But Hades moves forward and gestures for you to wait. He tells you it is time for his wife to return to the world above and offers you the honor of escorting her there. You bow and accept with gratitude.

Persephone rises from her throne, and with a parting kiss Hades sits in her place. The goddess takes your hand and together you walk through the dark, up toward the world above. The moment you take her hand you feel lighter, you can feel a spring breeze on your skin, smell the scent of a thousand blooming flowers, and a joyful laugher bubbles up inside you, the kind that fills you on a lazy summer day. Even here, crowned in iron, among the dead, Persephone is full of life. She smiles at you, knowing what you must feel.

"You wonder why I choose to dwell here? Why I ate the pomegranate seeds? Was I tricked or did I eat them willingly?" She gestures one hand to the tunnel you walk through. "Life needs rest. Every seed must germinate in the darkness of the soil before it may bloom. The darkness is not to be feared. You know this or you would not have traveled to this realm. My mother would have endless summer, but I know there is not wisdom in that. Without a time to rest, without the time to germinate and look within, the fruit of summer loses its sweetness. I chose to eat the seed, as I choose to walk these halls. The underworld was not thrust upon me, but a path I chose willingly. I would have it no other way."

Soon you see the dusky light of the world above and you and Persephone emerge from the underworld. As she steps upon the earth, flowers and other plants begin to bloom at her touch.

"From the fertile darkness I emerge renewed. And when I need to go to darkness again I will return." She cups your face with her hands and kisses your brow. "Do not fear the dark. It is needed, and when you need to go within and dwell in your own darkness so that you may make your life fertile on your return, come to my realm and seek wisdom at my throne." And with that the goddess vanishes.

You feel a new warmth in the air. Spring is in full bloom. But you know winter will come too in its time. And you know when you need to seek Persephone's wisdom, you will be able to find her again.

Persephone is the Greek goddess of spring and the queen of the underworld, who brings comfort and judgment to the dead. She is usually portrayed robed holding a sheaf of grain, alongside her mother Demeter, whom she was worshipped in conjunction with. Her origins seem to be that of a chthonic deity connected to agriculture. A plate found in Phaistos that dates to the Bronze Age may be one of the earliest depictions of Persephone, showing a goddess growing out of the ground with dancing girls and flowers around her.[47] Her husband, Hades, rules over everything below the ground as well as the unworldly, and it makes sense that his wife, representing the fertility of spring, would be connected to the fertility of the soil.

She was conflated with Despoina, an old chthonic goddess originating in Arcadia. According to Homer, Persephone was the daughter of the harvest goddess Demeter and Zeus, the king of the gods. Although if we consider her the same goddess as Despoina, she would be the daughter of Demeter and Poseidon. Demeter, taking the shape of a mare, had been pursued by Poseidon, and from their union she bore Despoina, originally in the form of a mare, and Areion, a mythical horse.[48] *Despoina* is essentially a title, meaning "mistress," as the true name of the goddess could not be revealed to anyone except those initiated into her mysteries.[49]

In Arcadia Demeter was worshipped alongside her daughter Despoina, making Despoina likely another name for Persephone or another incarnation of the goddess, as Persephone is also referred to as Kore at times, which means "girl" or "maiden" in Greek. It has been suggested that Kore represents the goddess of spring prior to her abduction, while Persephone is used to describe her only as Hades's bride. Ancient texts are not consistent in the use of these two names, however, and it seems more likely that the worship of Demeter and her daughter Kore merged at some point with the pre-Greek cultus of Persephone, perhaps because the two goddesses had similar stories and functions.

47. Walter Burkert, *Greek Religion*, trans. John Raffan (Cambridge: Harvard University Press, 1985), p. 42.

48. Pausanias, *Description of Greece*, vol. 4, trans. William Henry Samuel Jones and Henry Arderne Ormerod (Cambridge, MA: Harvard University Press, 1918), p. 25.

49. Burkert, *Greek Religion*, p. 280.

Persephone's abduction by Hades has several versions and is mentioned by Hesiod in the *Theogony* and in detail in the *Homeric Hymn to Demeter*. Zeus, her father, is a conspirator in her abduction: in the *Hymn* the king of the gods permits Hades to carry the young goddess off to his realm, perhaps fearing the overprotective Demeter would never let the girl marry. Hermes and Apollo both had courted Persephone, and Demeter had deemed both unworthy of her daughter and took her far from the other gods, presumably to keep her daughter safe. Persephone is picking flowers with her companions when Hades bursts through a cleft in the earth and takes her in his chariot to the underworld.

The ancient stories refer to the encounter as a rape and abduction, but this is only one way of viewing the story. At first glance Persephone seems like a victim of her circumstances and the power games of her godly parents. Neither Zeus nor Demeter take into account what the young goddess wants for her life. It would appear that Persephone's ability to choose is taken away, yet in my opinion her story has everything to do with choice. Like any myth, there are many ways to look at it, and any point of view has merit and meaning one can take from it. Sometimes we can't control what life throws at us or the deceptions of others, but how we choose to react to these challenges is vitally important.

Demeter mourned the loss of her daughter and searched for her all over the earth with Hekate's torches. Demeter demands Zeus have her daughter returned and relinquishes her blessing on the land, making it barren. Eventually, Zeus sends Hermes to Hades to demand the goddess be released to appease her mother, but before she leaves, Persephone eats a handful of pomegranate seeds. In the *Hymn to Demeter* Hades tells her she may return to her mother but that if she remains his wife, she will not only be a queen but become powerful among the gods: "I shall be no unfitting husband for you among the deathless gods, that am own brother to father Zeus. And while you are here, you shall rule all that lives and moves and shall have the greatest rights among the deathless gods: those who defraud you and do not appease your power with offerings, reverently performing rites and paying fit gifts, shall be punished for evermore." At these words, "wise Persephone was filled with joy and hastily sprang up for gladness." As a kind of insurance policy, Hades also "secretly gave her sweet pomegranate seed to eat, taking care for himself that she might not remain continually with grave, dark-robed Demeter." [50]

Hades knows that anyone who eats the food of the underworld may not leave it, and the other gods cannot deny his claim that Persephone must dwell in Hades's realm for part of the year having eaten its food. While Persephone dwells in the world above, there is spring and summer, and when she returns to Hades in mourning, Demeter again takes back her blessings on the land, causing winter.

When Persephone returns to her mother, Demeter questions her, expecting to hear about the other gods' deceit. She tells her mother that Hades forced her to eat the seeds. But I wonder if that is true. Does Hades ensure his wife's return by force? Or does she willingly eat the seeds, choosing to claim the power he speaks of? In many ways, she is choosing to make the best of a bad situation. She chooses in that moment to forge her own path, to take power over something that could have broken her. To not let her mother or Zeus choose for her. She enters the underworld a naive girl and leaves it as its queen.

At first glance this story gives us an explanation for summer and winter, but the cycle of the seasons is just one layer of the story. Persephone's story is perhaps the more quintessential story of the journey through the underworld. Like the reluctant hero, she is abducted, forced to travel to the underworld without having a choice. And in one of prime examples of the descent, she is forced to give us something by visiting the underworld: her innocence. Her mother's sorrow leads to a bargain, and she is able to return every half year.

Persephone's myth is not only an explanation for the cycle of the year, but also the cycles of our own lives and how we move through change. While there are at times big traumatic events, like her abduction, that shape us, we are constantly moving through change and transformation. It's an unending cycle. The person we were five, ten years ago is not the same person we are now. Persephone's willingness to return to the underworld and then to the world of the living shows that she knows she must work through times of change and undergo the mysteries of the underworld at periods of time. If she does not, then she cannot grow. She cannot enjoy the world above to its fullest. She

---

50. Evelyn-White, *Homeric Hymns and Homerica*, lines 360–74.

also enters the underworld as an initiate of their mysteries. She wears its crown on her head and is no longer the scared maiden. Once we have been dragged through the underworld kicking and screaming ourselves, it becomes easier to undergo the process in the future. We can accept change more readily; we know that we are strong because our mettle has already been tested. And we know the price. It is no longer the unknown to us. We know there are pain and difficulties, but we have walked the path before and we know we do not have to fear if we can weather the storm. We know there are rewards at the hard-fought end of our path.

Persephone embodies true ownership of self. She goes from someone who lets others make choices for her to the queen of her own domain and her own skin. She accepts change and sees that the months where the earth is fallow and bare are needed. Without those times, we cannot appreciate the spring or the fruitful seasons. There is also a burden attached to always being in full bloom. We get burnt out and need time to rest and to go within as Persephone does.

Devotional Work and Offerings for Persephone

Call on Persephone when you feel others are suppressing your ability to make your own choices and at times when you know you need to rediscover your inner self. Persephone's lessons are all about choice, both when our choices are taken from us and the moments when we take our power back from others and choose to change our stories. By all accounts, Persephone is loved by those she rules over. The choice of becoming Hades's wife was not her own, but as his queen she is an equal in power and a gatekeeper of the underworld in her own right.

She gives her favor to Heracles when he journeys to the underworld to capture Cerberus to complete his twelve labors. It is Persephone, enthroned beside her husband, who allows Orpheus the chance to retrieve his love Eurydice from the underworld. We tend to think of Persephone in terms of the young girl that gets carried away, as the maiden, and all the potential of spring, but that is only Persephone at the beginning of her story, not who she becomes at its end. When I work with Persephone, I do not feel the scared girl. She is all iron. She has a gentleness to her, but she is no less a queen. She sits upon her throne and rules with Hades at her side, owning her own path. She is no less the goddess of spring, but there is strength there that is not the maiden's. It is the feeling of someone who has earned their power and has come into their own. As queen of the underworld, Persephone holds dominion over choice, she becomes a gatekeeper to others, reminding us that while we can't always control our situations, we can choose whether to let those situations break us or transform them into something powerful.

Appropriate offerings for Persephone include flowers and pomegranates. A bouquet in a small vase on her altar is a simple but beautiful offering. As she is also the queen of the underworld, I like to use the dried flowers from her altar and add them to incense created in her honor. Once the flowers you have left for her have wilted, they can be hung outside or in a dark closet to dry. Once they are completely dried, they can be crushed and added to incense or magickal workings involving her. Honey or mead (honey wine) is also a good offering. Seeds, as a representation of potential and springtime, can also be used as offerings. If you are planning on planting a garden in the springtime, leaving the packets of seeds you intend to use on her altar until you are ready to plant is a nice way to add her blessings to a garden and honor her through your cultivation of the land.

················
Invocation to Persephone

Persephone
Maiden of spring
Iron-crowned queen
You rule over your own heart
You walk into the darkness of Hades
Your light never wavers
Your beauty shines even more brightly among the shades
And when you return with spring
You return with wisdom from the dark
Be with me now, mighty queen!

················
Ritual to Persephone to Forge a New Path

You Will Need:
Pomegranate
Black candle

If you cannot find a whole pomegranate, the seeds that are often sold separately in the health food aisle will do. Pomegranate juice can be a substituted offering as well. Light the candle and invoke Persephone in whatever manner you choose. When you feel her presence, say,

Persephone
You who ate the pomegranate
Seeds that won you a crown
Won you independence
Persephone
I take the course of my life in my own hands
I willingly walk unknown paths
Guide me as Hekate guides you through the dark
That I may rule my own path
Persephone
Iron-crowned queen
Help me in this task

See the task before you. Maybe it's claiming your independence, getting a new job, starting out on something new in life. Ask Persephone for her aid in helping you accomplish the task. When you are done, eat some of the pomegranate seeds and leave the rest as an offering to Persephone.

Persephone Spell of Fruition

You can use this to ask for Persephone's blessing in a literal garden, to enrich the soil and ask for the plants to grow healthy, or in the less literal sense for the fruition of a project.

You Will Need:

Seeds

Red wine

Pomegranate

This spell can be used to bless seeds you are planning on planting or a garden with plants already growing in it. If you are blessing seeds, have them on your altar when you begin.

If you are asking for a healthy garden, you can do this outside. Invoke Persephone and pour the wine on the ground near the center of the garden as an offering to her. Take the pomegranate and cut it in half, saying,

Lady of Spring
You who ruled the fertility of the soil
Whose touch brings forth flowers and grain
Persephone, bless the work I do
Let it bloom to fruition

Bury the pomegranate in the ground. Visualize the garden and plants growing healthy and full.

If the spell is for a project, do the same in front of your altar or in an outdoor place. Pour the wine in an offerings bowl instead, and bury the pomegranate in the ground near your home.

Conclusion: Walking the Path

*I*t is twilight and the sun is just beginning to set as you walk through a mist-covered wood. The path is old and worn and is familiar to you somewhat, as is this place. In some spots the mist clears and you can see farther ahead. There are some nooks and meadows that seem inviting and comfortable, while other areas are riddled with thorns that frighten you. As you walk the path, the mist clears and you see the entrance to a cave.

The cave's mouth is large and cavernous, with jagged rocks. You can see that the path continues straight into that gaping black maw. Take a moment to really look at the cave. Reach out a hand and feel the stone. Is it rough or smooth? Cold or warm? You look into the darkness within and can just make out steps carved into the rock before they get swallowed up into utter darkness. That darkness scares you. You don't know where the path through this cave will lead or what else may be within it. Do you continue on into the dark? There is no way to go around the cave. You could go back, you tell yourself, in the other direction. That path is familiar, comfortable if not unpleasant at times. But part of you knows there is no going back.

Then something moves in the darkness of the cave, and you take a terrified step backward, your heart racing. It is almost like all the darkness within the cave's maw is moving and condensing into a silhouette before the entrance. And soon the swirling darkness forms the figure of a woman. She is tall and regal, her skin, hair, and clothes all the color of the cave's blackness, as if she is nothing more than wisps of shadow woven together. The only thing that is not the color of shadows is a mask that she wears. It is pale white and almost looks like it is carved out of bone. The mask's face is blank and expressionless, and you wonder what the woman looks like underneath. The goddess moves like dark water, fluid like sooty smoke. And she reaches a hand toward *you, but you are still too afraid to take it. You know this is the dark goddess, the goddess of the underworld, the one who rules nightmares and battles, who reigns queen over the spirits of the dead. She is beautiful, but all she represents terrifies you.*

She extends her hand farther, and you wonder if she will grasp your hands and pull you down into the depths of the cave, willing or not, if you do not do what she wants.

"I am very patient," she says. "It is you who have come to my doorstep, whether you realize it or not. It is time, child. There can be no more waiting. No more stalling. Your path has led you here, to me, to the challenges you must face to become whole."

You look into the cave again and at the goddess, who is more than willing to guide you down, down into those depths, and the fear begins to well up inside you. You have been avoiding this place for a long time. You could have come here before, started this journey sooner, but you chose not to. Your heart races and the fear builds almost to the point that you think about turning and running. But the dark goddess shakes her head slowly, and she reaches out and grasps your hand. But it is not in anger as you had imagined. Instead it is a firm but gentle touch, and the touch of her warm skin eases the fear and calms you. She may be made of shadows, but her presence is towering and feels as solid and unmovable as granite.

"You do not fear me. What you fear is yourself. The monster that hides in the dark is nothing more than your own shadow. What does not conform or bend, what is in you that does not question—that is what lurks in the shadows. Your fearless, daring self. What rages and wails, what shines brightest, what hopes. This is what is locked away in the depths of that cave. Not the demons you imagine. Your sharp edges have been blunted, you have become complacent, handing your power to others, forgetting who you truly are."

Unsure where you find the bravery to do so, you reach up and touch the mask. The goddess stands close now, her face only inches from your own. And you pull the mask off and see your own face looking back at you.

The goddess smiles at you with your own face. "I will not promise you that the journey will be easy," she tells you, "But I will promise that I will be with you, I will be at your side through every step in the dark, and we will learn together who you will become." And with that the goddess dissolves back into the darkness of the cave.

You take one last look at the sun as it slips below the horizon, and with a deep breath you take the first step into the darkness. Each step brings you deeper and deeper into the earth. Deeper and deeper within your own darkness. And they seem like one and the same. You know as you descend into the darkness and feel the cold stone walls that surround you with outstretched hands that this is the same underworld that others have braved. And yet there is something personal about it as well. Your own demons live here too. Your own shadow roams these caverns. Part of you has always dwelt here and always will.

After some time, you take a moment to look back toward the entrance and realize the light that you thought might still be a distant, reassuring pinprick is gone. There is nothing but blackness behind you and nothing but hungry blackness before you. For the first time your steps falter just a little bit. A sudden fear surrounds you and begins to work its way up to your heart. You are truly alone. There is no way out but forward. Any illusions that you could go back have vanished with that light.

The fear within you rises even more when you hear something in the dark. You have stopped moving for the moment, and without your own footfalls echoing through the cave, you now hear someone else's. They are slow, heavy footfalls, but they are definitely coming toward you. Whatever it is, it's coming closer with every heartbeat, and still you cannot see what it is. The fear inside you builds to a panic, and, slightly ashamed of yourself, you turn to run back to the cave's entrance. Only, when you turn, the tunnel you just came from is gone. Desperately, you feel with your hands in the dark and realize there is a solid wall behind you now, although you were sure it was not there a moment ago.

Then there is a shift in the darkness. It is not the light of an entrance but instead the flowing, moving darkness of the goddess you met at the cave's mouth. She looks at you, her features a woman's, but the skin is dark and seems to move, like it is made of the night sky filled with stars, somehow bent and formed into the shape of a woman.

"You have made your choice. You have stepped into the dark, and now you must face it, and face it within yourself. There is no way back. You can choose to move forward, or you can choose to cower and let the underworld consume you. I will be with you. But the battles are your own to face. Which do you choose?"

And with that she fades back into the darkness, although her words stay with you. What will you choose? You couldn't stand still at the entrance to the cave, and now in its depths, more terrified than you have ever been, can you any less stand still? You must see this through to the end. You cannot stop till you reach the world above again. Standing still in the underworld means death.

Still terrified, you turn around. You listen for the footfalls coming toward you and you run toward them.

It takes only a few moments for you to come to the source of the sound. It is not the monster you thought would be there. It is dark, but not like the goddess. While she was made of stars, this thing before you, torch in hand, is human-shaped but made of dense, sticky darkness. The energy around it feels heavy and not at all like the night sky that made up the goddess who guided you here. When it speaks, you hear your own voice. It is not so much one voice but a chorus of voices. Every horrible thing you have thought about yourself, every critique, every doubt that has ever plagued you echoes around in the tunnel. In its shadowy darkness you see everything you are ashamed of in yourself. Every imagined transgression, everything you have been told you should not feel or want—this being is made up of all those things. The voices become louder around you, drowning out all other thoughts, becoming deafening. And you crouch down on the floor of the cavern almost overwhelmed. The smallest part of you that can still think hears the goddess's words again: "There is no way back. You can choose to move forward, or you can choose to cower and let the underworld consume you. Which do you choose?"

And you realize this is your shadow. It is a being of your own creation, one that only holds power over you if you allow it to. Slowly, you get up. And you look at the shadow and see it for what it is. Arms outstretched, you embrace it. It makes no move against you. Perhaps it is as surprised as you are. You embrace it, hugging it close to yourself, without shame and without disgust. And soon you feel its own arms embracing you as well, until the dark figure begins to melt into yourself and you are left holding the torch it held, an arm wrapped around yourself.

The goddess steps out of the shadows once again. "There are more challenges, more demons for you to face ahead. But face them not as a shattered, splintered being. You have embraced your shadow. Remember that you are enough, just as you are. The gods do not require perfection, only that you strive to be better with every step and every breath of existence."

With arms outstretched you continue onward and feel your way through the darkness of the cavern. You have faced many challenges, heard the encouraging voices of your guides and guardians as they watch you from the darkness. You no longer feel the paralyzing fear that gripped you when you first entered the cave to the underworld. That darkness almost feels comforting, and you feel different somehow. There may be more challenges ahead, but that knowledge does not make your steps falter or make you walk any slower through the caverns. You will meet what comes, whatever it is.

After some time, you see sparks of light in the distance. Is it the way out? You walk quickly toward it. Little sparks appear, then vanish, and then appear again. And soon you see as they ap-

pear that there are a face and hands illuminated by the sparks. An old woman sits in front of a pile of twigs and logs and is trying to light a fire. Soon you are right next to her and ask what she is doing. You thought there was no light in the underworld. In your entire journey there has only been the barest of illumination. A sliver of moonlight to illuminate the utter darkness. But that is not the same as a fire, and you long to see brilliant flames dancing in a merry fire. And it makes you long for home and beautiful nights when the darkness was illuminated by bonfires and the laughter of friends filled your ears.

The woman looks at you and smiles. She welcomes you to sit beside her. Her face is lined and etched with deep wrinkles that make her look kindly when she smiles. "There is more than shadow in the underworld. Fire can illuminate even the deepest darkness." She sparks the flint again; tiny sparks fly into the air but do not catch. She sighs. "After all, isn't that why you are here? Or were you planning on walking blindly through the underworld the whole time?"

She laughs at what must be your mouth hanging open. It may be dark, but she can see easily in the darkness, apparently. "Yes, part of the journey must be made in the darkness, facing it and walking blindly despite the fear. But you did not come here to learn to dwell in darkness, but to find the light that will illuminate it. How else can you understand the dark?"

You point out that even she has not been able to light her twigs. What chance do you have of building a fire?

"That is because I cannot light that fire, dear," she tells you. "I can show the way, I can inspire the sparks, but it is you who need to make the flames catch. You must stir the fires within you. You have let them burn down to mere embers until now. Will you stir them? Will you allow yourself to burn brightly? Will you allow the flames within you to drive you and empower you? Or will you walk in the dark forever? Yes, you no longer fear it, and that is good. There may yet be times you walk through these dark halls again, seeking answers, but you were never meant to dwell here forever."

She hands you the flint. And you close your eyes and see that banked fire that dwells in your own spirit as the woman says. All the dreams and desires you have put on hold, all the illusions you no longer believe that seemed so important at the beginning of your journey. You let that inner fire stir again. You let yourself want again, and hope again, and you see the fire grown stronger. You think about how strong you realize you are after your journey through the dark, the things you once feared and thought you could not do, that you now know are accomplishable. Stripped bare, you know now who you are more than you ever have. You see the embers within burst in a flame, and as you do you strike the flint and the sparks fly into the air. This time the twigs and logs catch fire easily. You blink and almost have to cover your eyes as the fire roars to life and illuminates the cavern tunnel. You were not scared of it before the fire was lit, but not being afraid of something is different from seeing it for what it is, knowing the shape of it, and seeing it with your own eyes in the light.

The old woman smiles at you. "Good! Very good," she tells you. She reaches in her robes and hands you a torch. "It is time to return now. Light the torch with your fire and you will find the way. But I warn you. Here in this place your fire is easy to see. It burns just as brightly in the world above, but there it is harder to see. In the daylight your fire is no less strong, but in the face of other light you will forget how brightly it shines against the darkness. You must be vigilant and not let it go out."

You promise to do so and thank her. As you walk through the illuminated cavern you soon see a pinprick of light in the distance. You run faster and faster until you find yourself at the opening of a cave, the sunlight pouring through as you climb up and up until you are on grassy earth, free of the underworld. You laugh and cry in happiness. And for a moment as you take in the beauty of the world above and feel the green grass between your fingers, you let the torch lie forgotten on the ground. You pick it up, and it still burns brightly. But you understand what the goddess meant. Here there is so much light. Your flame dances beautifully on the torch, but it seems small compared to the sunlight around you. It would be easy to forget how fierce and bright it shone in the darkness. You clutch the torch tightly, thinking again of those inner fires, and promise to tend them with care and let them burn brightly, not just in the dark but in the joyful sunlight and when things are happiest as well.

No matter how many times we encounter the lessons of the dark goddess, the path can be a difficult one. The reward is that we learn the depths of our souls and the faces of our truest selves. Working with the dark goddess in any of her guises changes us, sometimes in subtle ways, other times in drastic ones—we may look at ourselves not recognizing the person we have become after the whirlwind is over. In the journey we discover the nature of a part of the Divine Feminine that is like no other. Embracing the change the dark goddess gives us is an act of bravery. It is going into the dark of the underworld even though we are terrified. It is accepting that parts of ourselves will die so another can be born.

Each of the lessons has been different, and each of the faces of the dark goddess we have explored has changed my life in different ways. They have shown me that I am stronger than I ever imagined and that I have the power to change my life in amazing ways. And most of all they remind me to always strive to better myself. I cannot choose to be stagnant anymore. And just when I feel I have emerged for a time from the underworld and will never have to travel those paths again, they put new challenges in front of me, and the cycle begins all over again. Their lessons have been difficult, have changed me in so many ways that I cannot say I am the same person who began that journey with them so long ago. And I am grateful for it.

Whether you are just hearing the call of the dark goddess or have traveled her path before, I hope that she lights your way through the dark as she has illuminated mine and that you no longer fear the goddesses considered dark and dangerous. After all, living is a dangerous business. While her wisdom can be harsh, when we embrace the dark goddess, we learn to live life to its greatest potential and to become the best versions of ourselves.

Bibliography

Alvarado, Denise. *Voodoo Hoodoo Spellbook*. San Francisco: Red Wheel, 2011.

Amil, Segovia. *Ophelia Wears Black*. CreateSpace Independent Publishing Platform, 2015.

Aristophanes. *Plutus: The God of Riches*. Translated by Henry Fielding. Radford: SMK Books, 2011.

Atsma, Aaron J. "Hekate." The Theoi Project. Accessed May 15, 2017. http://www .theoi.com/Khthonios/Hekate.html.

Aubrey, John. *Remaines of Gentilisme and Judaisme*. Edited by James Britten. London: The Folk-Lore Society, 1881. https://archive.org/details/remainesgentili01aubrgoog.

Billinghurst, Frances. "Ereshkigal." In *Naming the Goddess*, edited by Trevor Greenfield. Winchester: Moon Books, 2014.

Bird, Stephanie Rose. *Sticks, Stones, Roots & Bones: Hoodoo, Mojo & Conjuring with Herbs*. St. Paul: Llewellyn Publications, 2004.

Black, Jeremy, Graham Cunningham, Eleanor Robson, and Gábor Zólyomi, eds. *The Literature of Ancient Sumer*. Oxford: Oxford University Press, 2006.

Boas, Franz. *The Central Eskimo*. Lincoln: University of Nebraska Press, 1972.

Burkert, Walter. *Greek Religion*. Translated by John Raffan. Cambridge: Harvard University Press, 1985.

Cavendish, Richard. *The Powers of Evil in Western Religion, Magic and Folk Belief*. London: Putnam, 1975.

Chödrön, Pema. "How to Move Forward Once You've Hit Bottom." *Lion's Roar: Buddhist Wisdom for Our Time* (blog), Oct 21, 2016. http://www.lionsroar.com/how-to-move-forward-once-youve-hit-bottom/.

Coburn, Thomas B. *Devī-Māhātmya: The Crystallization of the Goddess Tradition*. Delhi: Motilal Banarsidass, 2002.

Daimler, Morgan. "Irish-American Witchcraft: The Value of Our Shadow." *Patheos* (blog), February 2, 2016. http://www.patheos.com/blogs/agora/2016/02/irish-american-witchcraft-the-value-of-our-shadow/.

———. *Where the Hawthorn Grows: An American Druid's Reflections*. Winchester: Moon Books, 2013.

Davies, Sioned, trans. *The Mabinogion*. Oxford: Oxford University Press, 2007.

d'Este, Sorita, and David Rankine. *Hekate Liminal Rites: A Study of the Rituals, Magic and Symbols of the Torch-Bearing Triple Goddess of the Crossroads*. London: Avalonia, 2009.

Epstein, Angelique-Gulermovich. *War Goddess: The Morrigan and Her Germano-Celtic Counterparts*. Los Angeles: University of California Press, 1998.

Evelyn-White, Hugh G., trans. *The Homeric Hymns and Homerica*. Cambridge: Harvard University Press, 1914.

Fitch, Janet. *White Oleander*. New York: Back Bay Books, 2000.

Ford, Patrick K., trans. *The Mabinogi and Other Medieval Welsh Tales*. Berkeley, CA: University of California Press, 1977.

Foulston, Lynn, and Stuart Abbott. *Hindu Goddesses: Beliefs and Practices*. Eastbourne, UK: Sussex Academic Press, 2009.

Gager, John. *Curse Tablets and Binding Spells from the Ancient World*. New York: Oxford University Press, 1992.

Gane, Roy. *Cult and Character: Purification Offerings, Day of Atonement, and Theodicy*. Winona Lake, IN: Eisenbrauns, 2005.

Gray, Elizabeth. *Cath Maige Tuired: Second Battle of Mag Tuired*. Dublin: Irish Texts Society, 1983.

Gregory, Augusta, trans. *Gods and Fighting Men: The Story of the Tuatha De Danaan and of the Fianna of Ireland*. London: John Murray, 1905.

Helmsing, Clifton. *The Esoteric Codex: Deities of Night*. Lulu.com, 2015.

Hesiod. *Works & Days; Theogony*. Translated by Stanley Lombardo. Indianapolis, IN: Hackett Publishing, 1993.

Homer. *The Homeric Hymns: A New Prose Translation; and Essays, Literary and Mythological*. Translated by Andrew Lang. New York: Longmans, Green & Co., 1900. Reprinted by Amazon Digital Services, 2011. Kindle edition.

———. *The Iliad of Homer*. Translated by Richmond Lattimore. Chicago: University of Chicago Press, 1951.

Johnston, Sarah Iles. *Restless Dead: Encounters Between the Living and the Dead in Ancient Greece*. Los Angeles: University of California Press, 2013.

Kinsella, Thomas, trans. *The Tain: From the Irish Epic Táin Bó Cuailnge*. New York: Oxford University Press, 2002.

Kinsley, David. *Hindu Goddesses: Visions of the Divine Feminine in the Hindu Religious Tradition*. Los Angeles: University of California Press, 1988.

Kraig, Donald Michael. *Modern Magick: Eleven Lessons in the High Magickal Arts*. St. Paul: Llewellyn Publications, 2002.

Krasskova, Galina. *Devotional Polytheism: An Introduction*. Sanngetall Press, 2014.

Kübler-Ross, Elisabeth. *On Death and Dying: What the Dying Have to Teach Doctors, Nurses, Clergy and Their Own Families*. New York: Simon & Schuster, 2014.

Leahy, Arthur Herbert, trans. *The Courtship of Ferb: An Old Irish Romance Transcribed in the Twelfth Century into the Book of Leinster*. London: David Nutt, 1902. Facsimile by BiblioLife, 2009.

Lynch, Patricia Ann. *Native American Mythology A to Z*. 2nd ed. Mythology A to Z. New York: Chelsea House, 2010.

Masters, Robert Augustus. *Spiritual Bypassing: When Spirituality Disconnects Us from What Really Matters*. Berkeley, CA: North Atlantic Books, 2010.

McBeath, Hugh. *The Esoteric Codex: Titans.* Lulu.com, 2016.

McColman, Carl, and Kathryn Hinds. *Magic of the Celtic Gods and Goddesses: A Guide to Their Spiritual Power.* Pompton Plains, NJ: New Page, 2005.

Meredith, Jane. *Journey to the Dark Goddess: How to Return to Your Soul.* Winchester, UK: Moon Books, 2012.

Messenger, Katrina. *Descent: A Journey for Women.* Lulu.com, 2011.

Meyer, Kuno, trans. "Wooing of Emer," *Archaeological Review* 1 (1888): 68–75, 150–55, 231–35, 298–307.

Moorman, Charles. *The Works of the* Gawain-*Poet.* Jackson: University Press of Mississippi, 1977.

Nietzsche, Friedrich. *Thus Spoke Zarathustra.* New York: Macmillan, 1896.

O'Hogain, Daithi. *The Sacred Isle: Pre-Christian Religions in Ireland.* Suffolk: Boydell Brewer Ltd, 1999.

Parker, Robert. *Miasma: Pollution and Purification in Early Greek Religion.* Oxford: Clarendon Press, 1996.

Parker, Will, trans. *The Four Branches of the Mabinogi.* Dublin: Bardic Press, 2007.

Patton, Kimberly C. *The Sea Can Wash Away All Evils: Modern Marine Pollution and the Ancient Cathartic Ocean.* New York: Columbia University Press, 2007.

Pausanias. *Description of Greece.* 4 vols. Translated by William Henry Samuel Jones and Henry Arderne Ormerod. Cambridge, MA: Harvard University Press, 1918.

Pausch, Randy. *The Last Lecture.* New York: Hyperion, 2008.

Pollan, Michael. *The Omnivore's Dilemma: A Natural History of Four Meals.* New York: Penguin, 2006.

Puckle, Bertram S. *Funeral Customs: Their Origin and Development.* London: T. Werner Laurie, 1926. Reprinted by CreateSpace Independent Publishing Platform, 2013.

Rowling, J. K. "Text of J.K. Rowling's Speech." *Harvard Gazette*, June 5, 2008. http://news.harvard.edu/gazette/story/2008/06/text-of-j-k-rowling-speech/.

Verma, Preeity. *Small Changes, Big Difference: 7 Ideas for Personal Transformation.* Gurgaon: Partridge India, 2014.

Williamson, Marianne. *A Woman's Worth*. New York: Random House, 1993.

Zair, Nicholas. *Reflexes of the Proto-Indo-European Laryngeals in Celtic*. Brill's Studies in Indo-European Languages & Linguistics. Boston: Brill, 2012.

Index

To Write to the Author

If you wish to contact the author or would like more information about this book, please write to the author in care of Llewellyn Worldwide Ltd. and we will forward your request. Both the author and publisher appreciate hearing from you and learning of your enjoyment of this book and how it has helped you. Llewellyn Worldwide Ltd. cannot guarantee that every letter written to the author can be answered, but all will be forwarded. Please write to:

Stephanie Woodfield
⁒ Llewellyn Worldwide
2143 Wooddale Drive
Woodbury, MN 55125-2989

Please enclose a self-addressed stamped envelope for reply,
or $1.00 to cover costs. If outside the U.S.A., enclose
an international postal reply coupon.

Many of Llewellyn's authors have websites with additional information and resources. For more information, please visit our website at http://www.llewellyn.com.